D1565504

The Lutheran Ethic

The Lutheran Ethic

The Impact of Religion on Laymen and Clergy

by Lawrence K. Kersten
EASTERN MICHIGAN UNIVERSITY

WAYNE STATE UNIVERSITY PRESS   DETROIT   1970

To my parents and my wife, Alice

2 84. 173
K476

157868

Contents

The Schism Between Laymen and Clergy
A New Approach to Sociological Study of Religion

Tables

Foreword

THE ASSOCIATION of religion with the good, the beautiful, the honorable, the worthy is deeply rooted in the human consciousness. Indeed, in the minds of many the association is so strong as to brook no opposition. Religion by definition is good and, therefore, has not even the potential for evil.

The institutions of religion have benefited enormously from this widespread and pervasive imagery. The association of religion with the good underlies the special privileges which churches receive from government. It is also a major stimulus of the largesse bestowed on churches by their constituencies.

It would seem, given the size of the investment, that the churches would be under heavy pressure for periodic accounting to demonstrate that they are indeed the instruments for benevolence they are imagined to be. Such accounting is seldom called for and rarely, if ever, rendered. There is a widespread willingness to accept on faith that the church, like religion, is a good thing to have around.

History would seem to belie such idealization of the church's role. Examples of the church's capacity for malevolence abounds in every age. Such evidence, however, if it is acknowledged at all, tends to be dismissed as characteristic only of the church's past, not its present. In some people's views the church today is outdated, irrelevant, and impotent, but virtually no one believes that it is any longer harmful.

The Lutheran Ethic was not written, nor the research it reports undertaken, to test the assumption that the church is at its best benevolent and at its worst benign. The data collected, however, have the effect of producing such a test and the book, without Lawrence Kersten's intending it to be so, is an indictment of the church's benevolent imagery. Prejudice, chauvinism, insensitivity, selfishness, we discover, can also be the product of faith, even in contemporary times, unknowingly to those who profess it and who promulgate it.

There will not be consensus among readers about this indictment. There will be some who will not notice it, and many more who will not care. There will be others who will deny the evidence and still others who will see no malevolence in it. Such responses are not only possible but, given the tendency to idealize the church, probable. The challenge of the book for its Christian and especially Lutheran readers is whether these exhaust the responses it generates.

How the challenge is addressed will not decide the future of the church. But in a special, if small way, the response to *The Lutheran Ethic* will be a sign of what for the church the future portends. It deserves careful reading by those who care.

For those who do not care really any more and for whom sociological inquiry into religion is mostly of scholarly interest, the book also has its rewards, indeed rather considerable ones. That there is a Lutheran ethic distinct from that produced by the ascetic branches of Protestantism was noted by Max Weber, among others, many years ago. That the difference ever really counted has since been surmised. That it still counts and in ways markedly different from that usually attributed to the so-called Protestant ethic is a significant revelation of Kersten's inquiry. With time this book will be widely read in the scholarly community, and the rhetoric and the substance of the sociology of religion as they pertain to the ethical implications of faith will not be the same.

Charles Y. Glock
University of California at Berkeley

Preface

THIS BOOK explores the impact of religion on everyday life. It focuses on the distinctive religious ideology of Lutheranism and its influence on an individual's total world view and life organization. The research had two primary objectives. The first was determining the impact of religion on the attitudes and values of Lutherans in the three-county area of metropolitan Detroit. The study used five measures of religious commitment—beliefs, practices, knowledge, associational involvement, and communal involvement—which are described and contrasted throughout the book. An individual's degree of religious commitment is compared with his social, political, and moral attitudes.

A second objective was investigating the extent to which traditional Lutheran beliefs, attitudes, and behavior—the Lutheran ethic—remain viable in the secularized, urban culture of twentieth-century America. Ernst Troeltsch first used the term the Lutheran ethic in his work *The Social Teaching of Christian Churches* (tr. 1931), although Max Weber had discussed the basic elements of the ethic earlier in his *The Protestant Ethic and the Spirit of Capitalism* (1904). Weber and Troeltsch developed the Lutheran ethic from their analyses of the Lutheran Confessions and the writings of Martin Luther and Philip Melanchthon.

The Lutheran ethic goes beyond a statement of religious creeds and encompasses a total ideology—a complete weltanschauung or world view. It includes theological beliefs, social attitudes, and religious and nonreligious behavior. Contained in it are fundamental beliefs about God, man, eternal salvation, and the Bible. The ethic specifies roles for laymen, clergy, and the church. It sets guidelines for the institutions of the family, government, the economy, and education, as well as ideals about the social class structure in society.

The Lutheran ethic reflects life as it existed in the Middle Ages. In such a period life differed greatly from life in America today. For example, the social organization in which the state enforced the teachings of the church is quite different from the type of society in the United States, where the doctrine of separation of church and state prevails. Similarly, a rural society which opposed usury and capitalism contrasts dramatically with American society today which generally accepts the capitalistic norms that accompany its industrialized economy. Because religion is the most conservative institution in our society, however, it was expected that many of the ideological conceptions of the Lutheran ethic still endure, despite vast social changes over the last four hundred years.

In this study the Lutheran ethic functions as a theory to explain the data collected. In examining the findings the reader should bear in mind that the role of the sociologist is to study objectively what *is*, not to prescribe what ought to be.

The financial support for this study represents a new but long overdue approach to the sociological study of religion. It represents one of the few attempts of a major denomination to take an objective look at itself. The four Lutheran bodies involved in this study are to be commended for their willingness to participate in an in-depth analysis of their members, clergy, and churches. The entire research took approximately four years. During this period, the following sources provided financial support: the Board for Missions, the Lutheran Church—Missouri Synod; the Michigan District of the American Lutheran Church; the Detroit area congregations of the American Lutheran Church; the Social Action and Research Commission of the American Lutheran Church; the Board for American Missions of the Lutheran Church in America; the Michigan Synod of the Lutheran Church in America; the Detroit area congregations of the Wisconsin Evangelical Lutheran Synod; and the Lutheran Council in the United States of America.

The data came from three primary sources. The first was interviews with 886 Lutheran laymen living in the three-county area of metropolitan Detroit. The random sample of laymen was drawn from membership rolls of each of the four participating Lutheran bodies. A second source was a questionnaire completed by 241 Lutheran parish clergymen within the study area. The final source was a mailed questionnaire returned by 1,095 students of all faiths at Eastern Michigan University. This random sample made possible an investigation of religious and nonreligious differences between Lutherans and members of other denominations.

The four branches of Lutheranism involved in this study are the Lutheran Church in American (LCA) ; the American Lutheran Church (ALC) ; the Lutheran Church—Missouri Synod (MS) ; and the Wisconsin Evangelical Lutheran Synod (WS) .

I am indebted to the many students at Eastern Michigan University who helped in the pretesting of the research instruments, the coding of the data, and the analysis of the findings. The following students were involved: Corinne

Fine, Ruth Crum, Paul Hengehold, Sharon Graham, Diane
Jergens, Stephanie Hauptman, Jane Burger, Valerie Holt,
Susan Habib, Patricia Holt, Delois Whitaker, Brenda Gul-
lick, Leslie Kezlarian, Peggy Dunn, Le Ann Kayson, and
Marilyn Shillaire. In addition, the following Detroit area
students worked on the study: Sally Mars, Nancy Schliecher,
Jane Westacott, Ann MacKenzie, Cheryll McCaffrey, Robin
D'Ascenzo, Mary Hirzel, and Susan Heathfield.

The major burden of typing the many drafts of the interview schedule and questionnaires, as well as various drafts
of the manuscript, was handled by Eileen Keskeny. Myra
Gross handled recruitment, training, and supervision of the
interviewing process and also completed a major share of
the interviews herself. It would be impossible to name the
more than seventy-five or so dedicated interviewers who
made calls on more than 1,200 Lutheran households in the
Detroit area, but without their help this study would have
never been possible.

I am also indebted to the members of the General Com-
mittee of the Detroit Metropolitan Lutheran Research and
Planning Study who reviewed and criticized the study
throughout. This group included: the Rev. Charles Sand-
rock (ALC), the Rev. George Fleischer (ALC), the Rev.
Robert Wietelman (ALC), the Rev. Clarence Larson
(ALC), the Rev. Karl Boehmke (MS), the Rev. William
Woldt (MS), the Rev. Harold Hecht (MS), Donald Law-
rence (MS), James Cross (MS), the Rev. Paul Heinecke
(MS), the Rev. Eugene Beyer (MS), the Rev. E. C. Weber
(MS), the Rev. E. A. Westcott (MS), the Rev. Reuben
Schmidt (MS), Richard Jackson (LCA), the Rev. Ronald
Fuller (LCA), the Rev. Martin Yonts (LCA), Robert
Robinson (LCA), Harold Neilson (LCA), the Rev. Fred-
erich Marks (LCA), the Rev. Wayne Paterson (LCA), the
Rev. Wilmer Vallesky (WS), the Rev. Edward Zell (WS),

the late Rev. Frederich Schroeder (WS), and the Rev. Edwin Frey (WS).

In addition to these men, there were many other local clergymen who offered advice, criticism, and assistance in formulating questions. The three men who contributed the most were the Rev. Richard Feucht, the Rev. Richard Kapfer, and the Rev. Stephen Lippert. I am also grateful to Mel Ravitz of the Wayne State University faculty for his advice throughout the study. I received helpful comments and criticisms from other sociologists, including Charles Glock, Jeffrey Hadden, Gerhard Lenski, Benton Johnson, Ronald Johnstone, Thomas Hoult, and Raymond L. Schmitt. I am also grateful to Edward Green and Joseph Fauman, who were kind enough to read the manuscript and offer advice. The members of the staff of the Computing and Data Processing Center at Wayne State University provided helpful advice and service throughout the data processing phase. Particularly, the patient guidance and direction given by Barbara Wolfe was invaluable. Finally, as is true of most major undertakings in life, one owes most to those closest to him. In my case it was my wife, Alice, who gave me confidence and moral support when I needed it most, and who remained patient and understanding during the months and years of this vast undertaking.

L. K. K.

I

Introduction: The Lutheran Ethic

MAX WEBER's *The Protestant Ethic and the Spirit of Capitalism,* a classic analysis of religion and the socioeconomic values that emerged between the seventeenth and nineteenth centuries, has provided a base for much research and theory in the sociology of religion.[1] Lutheranism, the initial religion of the Reformation, has received far less attention than Calvinism, although Lutheranism provided part of the initial stimulus for the Protestant orientation toward capitalism. Moreover, the ethic of Lutheranism differs in many ways from the predominantly Calvinistic Protestantism described by Weber.

This study investigates the influence of the Lutheran ethic—a theological orientation distinct from Calvinism, Catholicism, and Judaism—on the beliefs, attitudes, and values of American Lutheran laymen and clergy in the four major branches of Lutheranism, the American Lutheran Church, the Lutheran Church in America, the Lutheran Church—Missouri Synod, and the Wisconsin Evangelical Lutheran Synod (ALC, LCA, MS, and WS). The data support the conclusion that the traditional Lutheran ethic continues to be a viable orientation in modern society, especially among the laity and clergy from the theologically more conservative branches of Lutheranism.

The Lutheran ethic emphasizes a particular image of man—that man was without sin only prior to the temptation of Adam and Eve. The Fall destroyed man's previously perfect nature, and he became a totally depraved being. Because of man's inherently evil nature, he is incapable of doing good by himself. The powerlessness of man, stressed by Martin Luther, contrasts with the traditional Roman Catholic belief that although man is born sinful, he may overcome this state by good works. The *Book of Concord,* a summary of the confessions and doctrines of Lutheranism, states that "original sin in human nature is not only a total lack of good in spiritual, divine things, but that at the same time it replaces the lost image of God in man with a deep, wicked, abominable, bottomless, inscrutable, and inexpressible corruption of his entire nature in all its powers, especially of the highest and foremost powers of the soul in mind, heart, and will."[2]

One of Luther's most famous works, *The Bondage of the Will,* describes man as having no free will, especially in regard to spiritual matters. "For if we believe it to be true that God foreknows and foreordains all things . . . and that nothing happens but at his will . . . then, on reason's own testimony, there can be no 'free-will' in man, or angel, or in any creature."[3] The *Book of Concord* indicates that man does have some free will in "external" or "nonspiritual" matters "to choose among the works and things which reason by itself can grasp." On the other hand, it points out great limitations of this freedom because of man's innate evilness. Men are found to "obey their evil impulses more often than their sound judgment, while the devil, who as Paul says (Eph. 2:2) is at work in the ungodly, never stops inciting this feeble nature to various offenses. For these reasons even civil righteousness is rare among men."[4]

The present study reveals little uniformity in beliefs about the original nature of man among the clergy and laity of the four branches of Lutheranism. In fact, in regard to most all beliefs, a single, unified Lutheran weltanschauung does not exist in the United States. Nevertheless, the theologically more conservative individuals (those belonging to the Missouri and Wisconsin synods, for the most part) more closely approximate the teachings of the traditional Lutheran ethic, and this orientation strongly influences their views on a large number of secular matters. A conservative theological stance relates to a conservative position on both religious and secular questions. The theologically conservative respondents are also more pessimistic than optimistic about the potentials of man in this world and see man's free will as severely restricted, both in this world and in the next. The theologically liberal laymen and clergy take a more optimistic view of man, and in rejecting many of the elements of the Lutheran ethic they appear to be moving in the direction of the beliefs and attitudes of most other major Protestant denominations in the United States.

Salvation, according to the Lutheran ethic, comes only as a free gift of grace from God, through Jesus Christ, and is not affected by the worldly deeds of men. Man is assured of salvation by grace alone *(sola gratia)*. His efforts do not pay for or add to his salvation. Luther asserts: "For God wants to save us not by our own but by extraneous *(fremde)* justice and wisdom, by a justice that does not come from ourselves and does not originate in ourselves but comes to us from somewhere else."[5] Although both Catholicism and Lutheranism adhere to a doctrine of grace, Lutheranism deemphasizes the church hierarchy, religious rituals, and works of merit that are regarded as important steps in gaining grace for Catholics. Thus, for Lutherans grace and salvation cannot be "obtained" through church authorities. Faith and the possibility of salvation are more individual and personal.

In comparison to Calvinism, the Lutheran ethic holds

that the church is more directly involved in the process of receiving grace. The doctrine of predestination, one of the basic tenets of Calvinistic theology, assumes that God predestines some individuals to receive grace and others to be damned. Weber points out that in Lutheranism, however, grace is freely given to those who trust in God. Grace is considered to be revocable, but can be received again "by penitent humility and faithful trust in the word of God and in the sacraments."[6] In Calvinism neither human merit nor the mediation of the church through the sacraments is considered to be a factor in receiving or losing grace; in Lutheranism, however, through Baptism, Holy Communion, and the proclamation of the Word the church becomes the channel through which grace is received.

Calvin believed that only a few would be chosen for eternal grace. But how is one to know if he is among the predestined elect? For the Calvinist "in order to attain that self-confidence, intense worldly activity is recommended as the most suitable means. It and it alone disperses religious doubts and gives certainty of grace." Worldly success itself is a sign of salvation for the Calvinist. Luther, on the other hand, indicates that grace will be given to all those humble sinners who will just "trust themselves to God in penitent faith."[7]

"Grace" and "salvation" in the Christian sense do not appear in the Jewish religion. The Jew already considers himself to be part of the "chosen people," and thus there is no need for him to seek grace or the assurance of salvation through a merit system emphasizing good works. Also, the Jews do not look upon the religious institution and hierarchy as a dispenser of grace, nor do they regard religious rituals or attendance at worship services as mandatory religious duties affecting salvation.

Although Lutheranism is usually considered to be a religion stressing the grace of God rather than the Law of God, Old Testament Law does make up an important segment of the Lutheran ethic. In fact, Luther has been accused of using the Old Testament as if it were a legal code.[8] He quite naturally turned to the Bible in seeking a system of ethics that could be used as an ideal standard for all people. However, the specific purpose of the Law is to act as a stimulus to repentance by pointing out man's sinful nature and helplessness. The majority of Lutheran laymen today, in contrast to their views of being saved by God's grace through faith and trust, also say that they are saved by keeping the Ten Commandments and living a good moral life. Luther's strong emphasis on the Law of God thus exists today despite the contradictory evidence of theology. A stress on moral conduct, based on Old Testament Law, is almost as much a part of the thinking of the individual Lutheran layman as is the concept of free grace.

In keeping with Luther's definition of the role and function of the church as "preaching the gospel," most Lutherans surveyed oppose efforts for social reform by the church. Little in Lutheran theology directs the church to attempt to build the kingdom of God in this world. Troeltsch writes that "down to the present time the Lutheran position is based essentially upon the religious theory of the purely spiritual nature and 'inwardness' of the Church, while all external secular matters are handed over to reason, . . . to the civil authority." In its emphasis on philanthropy and charity rather than social reform, Lutheranism tends to "alleviate but not recreate."[9] Such thinking is harmonious with the traditional Lutheran doctrine of the two kingdoms, with sharp distinctions between the spiritual and temporal worlds. Luther writes that "he who would confuse these two kingdoms as our false fanatics do would put wrath into God's kingdom and mercy into the world's kingdom; and that is the same as putting the devil in heaven and God in hell."[10]

According to Martin Luther, the goal of the individual Christian should be personal salvation, and this is the view held by most Lutherans today. The typical Lutheran still learns to be humble and to patiently endure existing conditions on earth. Although the ethic stresses that "works should follow from grace," the data of this study suggest that the concept is reflected only in a personal moral conduct based on, and limited to, Biblical law. No collective efforts toward social reform are considered desirable or necessary. Exceptions occur among theologically liberal clergymen, especially young clergymen, who stress the importance of church involvement in social action movements. Although most of the laity of the two liberal branches of Lutheranism (LCA and ALC) favor a noninvolvement stance, there is some evidence that college-aged Lutherans affiliated with the liberal branches see a greater role for the church in secular affairs. Negro Lutherans also favor considerably more social action on the part of the church and its leaders than do white Lutherans.

The individual Lutheran's role in society is determined primarily by Luther's concept of the calling. God calls an individual to carry out certain duties, and all callings have the same worth in the sight of God. The result is an earthly inequality, and a spiritual equality which is "the objective historical order of things in which the individual has been placed by God."[11] Since the social order is considered to be a direct manifestation of the divine will, Lutherans should make no attempt to change it. The role of the individual, according to the Lutheran ethic, is one of quietism and passivity toward the secular world. The conservatism concerning worldly matters results from the emphasis that Lutheranism places on trust in God, on the distrust of man's motives, and on the futility of his efforts. Since God's will is all that matters and man is by nature a self-centered, sinful creature who cannot be expected to solve worldly problems, it follows that patient endurance of this world and anxious anticipation of the next become the individual Lutheran's primary orientation.

Luther saw secular institutions as necessary to restrain wickedness in a sinful and temporal world. He believed that such institutions and the existing state of affairs were appointed and ordained by divine providence. War, government, violence, law, and property were all viewed as part of God's plan. Whatever the existing situation of the social order, man can be assured that it has its good side, inasmuch as it is a product of God's will. All that remains for the individual Christian is obedience and humble submission to these institutions. Troeltsch argues that classical Lutheranism needed the state to enforce its religious philosophy, but under changing political conditions such as the complete separation of church and state Lutheranism lost the means by which its theories could be forced into practice. "Unlike Catholicism and Calvinism, Lutheranism possessed no organ by which it could put its theories into practice apart from the State, and the modern State, for its part, no longer feels itself—as in early Lutheranism—to be the secular aspect of the organism of Christian Society. This was the beginning of the social impotence of Lutheranism, in so far as it had not adopted Calvinistic and modern ideas."[12] Because Lutheran doctrine conceives of government as being ordered by God, individuals should not actively seek to change it. Luther writes: "God would prefer to suffer the government to exist no matter how evil, rather than allow the rabble to riot, no matter how justified they are in doing so."[13] Consistent with the Lutheran ethic, Lutherans interviewed in this study overwhelmingly disapprove of civil disobedience. More importantly, a conservative theological stance relates strongly to conservative political attitudes of all types.

Despite the fact that the Lutheran ethic provides a patriarchal orientation toward family life, Lutherans today feel that women should have as much to say as men in both the family and the church. However, with the exception of the theologically liberal clergymen, other aspects of traditional Lutheran theology, such as an emphasis on obedience in childrearing and opposition to premarital and extramarital sexual relations, still receive strong support. On the other hand, only the theologically conservative clergymen follow Luther's negative views regarding birth control and divorce.

Luther did all he could to combat the new economic order of capitalism. For Luther the traditional agrarian medieval society had no place in it for the spirit of competition. He saw capitalism as "contrary to humility, to trust in God, to brotherly love, to Nature, and to God."[14] Tawney points out that Luther took an even more rigid stand than the Roman Catholics on usury.[15] Weber sees Lutheranism as distinctly differing from the Protestant ethic in terms of economic motivation. For the Lutheran, external activity in the world is not considered important or necessary. Such activity is regarded as a sign of a lack of faith in God and a lack of grace. For the Calvinist, on the other hand, economic activity and success in the world is one means by which an individual can assure himself that he is among those predestined to be saved. The difficulty of the growth of capitalism in predominantly Lutheran countries, the concentration of Lutherans in lower and middle class professions, and evidence of the lack of "success" of Lutherans in the world all indicate that the economic aspect of the Lutheran ethic has in the past and continues today to exert a strong restricting influence.

According to Troeltsch, Luther was not a strong supporter of scientific and secular education. Striving to fulfill the duties of one's calling is all that is asked by God. The result of this doctrine, according to Troeltsch, "was a terrible spiritual and intellectual sterility, which formed a glaring contrast to the social doctrines of Catholicism and Calvinism."[16] Luther opposed attempts to explain everything by the use of reason. The paradoxes in Lutheran theology are not to be comprehended on the basis of logic, but rather are to be accepted as unexplainable items understood only by God. Secular learning is insignificant in terms of God's plan. Intense intellectual interest is even considered as a possible sign of a lack of confidence in God's grace. Tawney points out that Luther suspected that the devil is somehow involved in the use of reason and learning.[17] Luther concluded that education naturally involves the use of reason and gives man a misguided self-confidence and arrogance. Such an attitude is contrary to the humble, submissive surrender and complete dependence upon God which Lutheran theology holds to be necessary to receive the free gift of grace. The data show that Lutherans today, except for theologically liberal clergymen, hold to nonscientific views regarding the origins of man and also see serious conflicts between science and religion.

Basic to the social class system outlined in the Lutheran ethic is the belief that differences in individual abilities do exist, and that fixed and unequal class positions are part of God's natural order. Since these inequalities in the existing class positions are God's will, they are not to be tampered with. In Lutheran theology, spiritual equality is the prime factor, and being materially poor in the world is not a great disadvantage. The Bible (Luke 6:20-24 and 18:22-25) gives strong encouragement to the masses on the lower levels of the social hierarchy and explicitly states that the poor have as much and possibly more opportunity to enter the kingdom of God after death.

Troeltsch has summarized Luther's views regarding social mobility: "It is against all law, both Natural and Divine, to wish to rise in the world, to break through existing institutions on one's own free initiative, to agitate and destroy Society by individual efforts, to improve one's manner of life, or to improve one's social position." Such views obviously helped to support a doctrine of slavery. "Serfdom . . . was regarded in precisely the same way as slavery was regarded in the Early Church, as a class, that is in which men may enjoy the inner liberty of Redemption, but in which they have no right to seek external legal freedom."[18] According to Tawney, Luther's opposition to attempts to abolish serfdom were "intensified by a political theory which exalted the absolutism of secular authorities and a religious doctrine which drew a sharp antithesis between the external order and the life of the spirit." Luther indicated that "an earthly kingdom cannot exist without inequality of persons. Some must be free, others serfs, some rulers, others subjects."[19] The data show that except among the theologically most conservative clergymen, Lutherans no longer look upon the class system as God-given and unchangeable by man, nor poverty as a necessary and enduring problem. However, the strong prejudices among Lutherans against particular minorities may well be reinforced by the Lutheran ethic view of social class and slavery.

According to Weber, the Lutheran ethic offers no real unified moral or ethical system. The primary moral obligation is absolute self-surrender in faith and trust to God. Luther disliked emphasizing behavior or morality because it seemed to border on good works. As far as he was concerned, attempts to externalize religion into laws, rules, and regulations only degrade it. This study supports the conclusion that the Lutheran ethical system is one of individual morality and piety. No group or communal concern is evident, the result being a strong emphasis on religious individualism. The ethic stresses trust and confidence in divine providence. The consequences of these ethical ideas are reflected in the social impotence of Lutheranism in the entire secular realm. Lutheran social philosophy suggests that true happiness for man and total release from the bondage of sin are not possible until after death. If earthly conditions are undesirable, man should patiently endure them, for they may actually be a test of his faith. Man must trust that God will change the social structure or social conditions when He sees fit. Pietistic indifference, which the Lutheran conception of the two kingdoms emphasizes, expresses itself in the lack of basic ethical commands in the world. As Niebuhr writes in commenting of Luther's social ethic, Luther "divided life into compartments, or taught that the Christian right hand should not know what a man's worldly left hand was doing."[20]

Weber states "Lutheranism, on account of its doctrine of grace, lacked a psychological sanction of systematic conduct to compel the methodical rationlization of life."[21] Lutheranism accepts an ideology of life stressing conservatism. Niebuhr suggests that if Lutheranism has "contributed to social change, this has resulted largely without its intention and not without the assistance of other groups. Conservatism is a logical consequence of the tendency to think of law, state, and other institutions as restraining forces, dykes against sin, preventers of anarchy, rather than as positive agencies through which men in social union render positive service to neighbors advancing toward true life."[22]

II

The Religious Commitment of Lutherans

AN IMPORTANT prerequisite to measuring the impact of the Lutheran ethic on secular attitudes and behavior was conceptualizing the independent variable of religion. In what ways can an individual's religiousness be theoretically distinguished and scientifically measured? This study built on previous conceptualizations of various manifestations of religiosity and sought to improve upon the typological models. The works of Glock, Fukuyama, Fichter, and Lenski[1] served as meaningful references.

The study centers on five dimensions of religious commitment: religious beliefs, religious practices, religious knowledge, associational involvement, and communal involvement. These five indicators encompass the major measurable aspects of religiosity. We investigated the lay and student samples on all five dimensions, but analyzed the clergy sample only for religious beliefs.[2]

Although the aspects of religious commitment used do not exhaust all of the possible types of religious orientations, for the objectives of this study the dimensions adequately cover an individual's religious commitment. These dimensions encompass the formal institutional or organizational aspect, the informal subcommunal group aspect, and the individual-personal aspects of religious commitment.

RELIGIOUS BELIEFS

The religious beliefs dimension is probably the most important expression of religious commitment. It is on the basis of beliefs, particularly as they relate to the meaning and purpose of life, that individuals form basic values and attitudes. Religious beliefs in this study are measured by the respondents' answers to four questions regarding traditional Christian teachings. The first question tests how the individual views the Bible (Table 2-1). In the other three questions Lutherans gave an agree, probably agree, probably disagree, or disagree response to statements relating to literal or nonliteral interpretations of the Bible (Table 2-2).

The data show that widely varying belief patterns exist among the branches of Lutheranism. Differences are also apparent, although in somewhat varying degrees, between laymen and clergy. In general, these patterns of differences will reappear throughout the book. The Wisconsin Evangelical Lutheran Synod (WS) is the theologically most conservative, and the clergy from this body agree unanimously on the four religious belief questions. The Lutheran Church—Missouri Synod (MS) is almost as conservative, but there are trends toward change. The American Lutheran Church (ALC) is more liberal, while the Lutheran Church in America (LCA) is generally the most liberal.

In almost every instance the MS and WS laity give considerably more liberal responses than the MS and WS clergy on the four belief questions. Within the LCA and ALC the reverse is true, except for the question on original sin. Thus, at least in relation to theological beliefs, the MS and WS clergy represent a conservative influence on their laity, and the LCA and ALC clergy a liberalizing influence.

On the first question the percentages of laymen choosing the theologically most conservative answer—"The Bible is

TABLE 2-1
Lay and Clergy Views on the Bible, By Branch of Lutheranism

| | Sample | By Percentage | | | |
		LCA	ALC	MS	WS
The Bible is God's word and all it says is true (theologically most conservative)	Lay*	29	35	62	77
	Clergy*	10	19	74	100
The Bible was written by men inspired by God, and its basic moral and religious teachings are true, but because the writers were men, it contains some human errors.	Lay	47	47	27	16
	Clergy	76	74	18	0
Even though the Bible contains many errors and myths, it still represents God's teachings.	Lay	24	17	10	7
	Clergy	12	7	4	0
Don't know	Lay	0	1	1	0
	Clergy	2	0	4	0

Lay — $\chi^2 = 137.8024$
$df = 9, p = .001$
Clergy — $\chi^2 = 103.5031$
$df = 9, p = .001$
(Only levels of significance, p, will be given in future tables.)
*The number of lay and clergy varies only slightly throughout from totals in Appendix I.

God's word and all it says is true"—range from 29 percent in the LCA to 77 percent in the WS. The clergy responses are 10 percent in the LCA, 19 percent in the ALC, 74 percent in the MS, and 100 percent in the WS. The 90 percent difference between the LCA and WS clergymen seems almost inconceivable within the single denomination of Lutheranism. Although laymen do not approach the extremes of the clergy on this question, substantial differences emerge between the various Lutheran bodies.

The second question, relating to the Biblical account of Adam and Eve, finds a range from 48 percent of the LCA to 83 percent of the WS laymen giving the traditional Lutheran answer (disagree). The same liberal-to-conservative trend among the four Lutheran bodies on the first question appears here. Among the clergy the percentages giving a disagree response range from a low of 17 percent in the LCA to 100 percent in the WS.

On the question referring to the traditional Christian belief that "only those who believe in Jesus Christ as their Savior can go to heaven," the theologically most conservative answer is agree. Among the laymen from 56 percent in the LCA to 84 percent in the WS give the conservative response. Clergymen agreeing range from 43 percent in the LCA, 52 percent in the ALC, 84 percent in the MS, to 100 percent in the WS. Once again the clergy show greater differences than the laity.

On the question relating to the traditional Lutheran view of man's basic nature, the statement presented was: "A child is already sinful at birth." This covers the important doctrine of original sin, a key element of the Lutheran ethic. Laymen of all four branches take a more optimistic view of man's nature than the clergy, and the clergy answering agree range from 67 percent in the LCA to 100 percent in the WS. The trend reflecting significant theological differences among the four Lutheran bodies occurs again.[3]

The Religious Beliefs Index

The questions on religious beliefs were grouped to form a Religious Beliefs Index. The four questions in the index were considered to have the same importance and were weighted equally. This study used the same procedure throughout for the construction of indexes. In the Reli-

gious Beliefs Index, one point is given for the theologically
most conservative answer to each of the four questions.
Table 2-3 shows scores for the clergy and laity for each

TABLE 2-2
Lay and Clergy Religious Beliefs, By Branch of Lutheranism

| | | By Percentage | | | |
	Sample	LCA	ALC	MS	WS
The account of Adam and Eve fall-	Lay	48	59	81	83
ing into sinfulness is simply a story	Clergy	17	28	80	100
which did not take place in reality.					
(Disagree)*					
Only those who believe in Jesus	Lay	56	58	75	84
Christ as their Savior can go to	Clergy	43	52	84	100
heaven. (Agree)*					
A child is already sinful at birth.	Lay	45	58	77	79
(Agree)*	Clergy	67	74	96	100

$p = .001$ for all questions.

*Theologically most conservative response.

branch of Lutheranism. An individual who did not answer
one or more of the questions was not considered in the index. As a result, the number of respondents on any index
varies slightly from the total number of completed interviews and questionnaires.

The scores in Table 2-3 were collapsed into low, moderate, and high degrees of theological conservatism (Table
2-4). Those individuals with scores of 0 or 1 were categorized as ranking low and were considered to be the theologically most liberal. Individuals with scores of 2 and 3 were
ranked moderate, and only those who answered all four
questions with the most conservative answers, a score of 4,
were categorized as ranking high, the theologically most
conservative. Differences similar to those found on individual belief questions among the four Lutheran bodies and
between the laity and clergy appear on the index.[4] Appendix I considers the validity of the Religious Beliefs Index.

The distribution of laymen and clergy on the Religious Beliefs Index indicates a widely varying belief system within Lutheranism. Only among the clergy in the Wisconsin Synod does there seem to be any real consensus.

TABLE 2-3
Lay and Clergy Scores on the Religious Beliefs Index,
By Branch of Lutheranism

| Branch | Sample | N* | Low Theological Conservatism | | | High Theological Conservatism | |
			0	1	2	3	4
LCA	Lay	239	22	24	20	22	12
	Clergy	50	18	38	30	10	4
ALC	Lay	187	15	19	27	20	19
	Clergy	52	17	34	21	15	13
MS	Lay	221	6	8	14	29	43
	Clergy	112	3	7	11	16	63
WS	Lay	228	3	5	15	23	54
	Clergy	16	0	0	0	0	100

*The number of cases is the same throughout the study except for minor variations on individual questions.

For all other clergy and lay groups there seems to be as much difference within each of the Lutheran bodies as between them. Thus, a theologically liberal layman may hold membership in the Wisconsin Synod or a theologically conservative individual may belong to the LCA. For this reason subsequent chapters will compare secular attitudes and behavior by the theological stance of the individuals, as well as by branch of Lutheranism.

The data presented on the religious beliefs of Lutheran laymen and clergy are, of course, applicable only to the region studied. Two other studies show similar findings, however, and thus support the data. Hadden's national sample of clergymen from six major denominations allows a comparison of the belief patterns of Detroit area clergy with those of Lutheran clergymen in the entire United States.[5] Two Lutheran bodies, the American Lutheran Church and the Lutheran Church—Missouri Synod, were

TABLE 2-4

Lay and Clergy Rankings on the Religious Beliefs Index,
By Branch of Lutheranism

Branch	Sample	Low	By Percentage Moderate	High
LCA	Lay	46	42	12
	Clergy	56	40	4
ALC	Lay	34	47	19
	Clergy	51	36	13
MS	Lay	14	43	43
	Clergy	10	27	63
WS	Lay	8	38	54
	Clergy	0	0	100

$p = .001$

included in Hadden's study of Protestant clergymen. Hadden used the statement "Scriptures are the inspired and inerrant Word of God, not only in matters of faith but also in historical, geographical, and other secular matters" as opposed to this study's "The Bible is God's word and all it says is true." Hadden found 23 percent agreement among ALC clergy and 76 percent among MS clergy, as compared with 19 percent and 74 percent agreement, respectively, in this study. Hadden's question "I believe in the demonic as a personal power in the world" parallels this study's "I believe in the devil as an active and evil being in the world," and agreement responses were 86 percent (ALC) and 91 percent (MS) for Hadden, as compared to 78 percent (ALC) and 90 percent (MS) in this survey. Although the questions are worded somewhat differently, their meanings seem similar.

The beliefs of Lutheran clergymen in the Detroit area and the beliefs of Lutheran clergymen nationally show marked similarities, supporting the hypothesis that the clergymen from the various branches of Lutheranism hold belief systems emphasized during their seminary education, which, with minor regional variations, they retain no matter what part of the country they are called to serve.

Stark and Glock's sample of church members in Northern California permits a comparison of the religious beliefs of Lutheran laymen.[6] Again, although the wording of questions and answers in the two studies differs somewhat, the meaning is similar. Their data grouped together the ALC and LCA members, but the Missouri Synod was separate. Stark and Glock used the statement "A child is born into the world already guilty of sin," whereas this study used "A child is already sinful at birth." Stark and Glock found 49 percent of the LCA and ALC (combined) and 86 percent of the MS laymen saying the statement is true, while 45 percent of the LCA, 50 per cent of the ALC, and 77 percent of the MS laymen in this study agree with the statement. In the Stark and Glock sample 49 percent of the LCA and ALC and 77 percent of the MS said "The devil actually exists" compared with 58 percent (LCA), 66 percent (ALC), and 78 percent (MS) agreeing with the statement "I believe in the devil as an active and evil being in the world." Finally, Stark and Glock used the statement "Miracles actually happened just as the Bible says they did" as compared with "The miracles in the Bible did not actually happen in fact, but were stories used by Jesus in His teachings" in this study. In their survey 69 percent of the LCA and ALC and 89 percent of the MS agreed with the statement in comparison to 67 percent of the LCA, 71 percent of the ALC, and 79 percent of the MS in this study disagreeing with the statement.

Social Correlates of Religious Beliefs

Researchers have often suggested that such key social variables as age, sex, social class, and nationality relate to religious beliefs. The present study examined a number of these variables in relation to an individual's ranking on the Religious Beliefs Index.[7]

No differences appear between the laymen's age and his ranking on the Religious Beliefs Index. For the clergy, on the other hand, very significant differences appear, with younger clergymen more often ranking low (liberal) and older clergymen more often high (conservative). If the younger clergymen maintain their liberal theological beliefs through the years, then dramatic changes in Lutheran belief patterns likely will occur. (See Table A-1) *

Upper class Lutherans more often than lower class Lutherans have liberal religious beliefs (Table A-2). Social class was measured by a combination of income and education.[8] No differences exist in the rankings of the clergy according to the occupational structure of the minister's parish, which suggests that clergymen hold to religious beliefs systems independent of the social class of their congregations.

An individual is more likely to rank high on the index if he has ever attended a Lutheran parochial school. Of the respondents ranking most conservative 44 percent have attended a parochial school and 28 percent have attended public schools only.[9]

Laymen born outside of the United States are significantly more liberal theologically than those born in the United States. Thirty-eight percent of the laymen born in another country and 24 percent born in this country rank low on the belief index. Similarly, long-time residents of

America, as compared with more recent immigrants, generally rank higher, suggesting that theological conservatism increases with the Americanization process, at least through the third generation. Twenty-one percent of the first generation Americans, 30 percent of the second, and 33 percent of the third and fourth generations rank most conservative.

The type of community in which a Lutheran layman was reared also relates to his religious beliefs (Table A-3). The more rural the community, the more likely he ranks high on the index. Forty-two percent reared on a farm rank most conservative on religious beliefs, as compared to 28 percent brought up in a large city. The clergy show no significant differences in belief patterns by place of rearing.

How an individual became a member of the Lutheran church also makes some differences in his religious beliefs (Table A-4). The largest portion of laymen ranking high on the Religious Beliefs Index have been Lutherans since childhood (37 percent). The next most conservative group are individuals who converted to Lutheranism from no religious faith, excluding converts at marriage. These individuals are twice as likely to rank high (31 percent) as low (15 percent) on the index. Most likely to hold liberal beliefs are those who became Lutheran members through marriage (36 percent), and those who at one time fell away but later renewed their membership (36 percent).

Members of inner-city churches usually are slightly more liberal theologically than members of suburban churches.[10] A more marked trend exists among the clergy, where ministers with inner-city congregations more frequently rank low (50 percent) than suburban pastors (23 percent) on the Religious Beliefs Index. No significant differences occur in the belief patterns between Lutheran males and females. Also, nationality or race for either the laymen or clergy does not account for significant differences.

ASSOCIATIONAL INVOLVEMENT

A second dimension of religious commitment, associational involvement, refers to an individual's participation in the institutional life of the church. This dimension is dis-

TABLE 2-5
Lay Attendance at Religious Services in the Last Year,
By Branch of Lutheranism

Branch	(N)	Once a Week or More	2-3 Times a Month	Once a Month	A Few Times	Never
LCA	(241)	42	35	10	10	3
ALC	(192)	46	25	8	18	3
MS	(223)	56	28	6	7	3
WS	(229)	51	32	7	9	1

By Percentage

$p = .05$

tinct from the personal religious practices carried on outside the formal church organization.

Two measures in the survey gauged associational involvement—frequency of attendance at religious services in the last year and participation in activities or organizations of one's church other than formal worship services. The percentages of laymen attending religious services once a week or more is highest in the MS and lowest in the LCA (Table 2-5). On the second question no statistically significant differences exist among the four Lutheran bodies. In the WS more members participate in activities and organizations (57 percent), while the ALC has the lowest percentage (48 percent).

The Associational Involvement Index

Although it could be simply a chance variation, according

to the Association Involvement Index, members of the theologically more conservative Lutheran bodies (MS and WS) are more institutionally active than those belonging to the

TABLE 2-6
Lay Rankings on Associational Involvement Index,
By Branch of Lutheranism

Branch	Low	By Percentage Moderate	High
LCA	38	30	32
ALC	36	34	30
MS	30	30	40
WS	30	32	38

$p = $ NS

theologically more liberal bodies (LCA and ALC). The two questions measuring associational involvement were used to develop this index.[11] The differences found here do not reach statistical significance, but slight variances appear between each of the four Lutheran groups in the low and high categories (Table 2-6).

Social Correlates of Associational Involvement

Social class varies significantly with associational involvement (Table A-5). A higher social class of a layman results in a higher ranking on the index. Thus, while only 28 percent of the lower class Lutherans rank high, 46 percent of the upper class rank high. As in the analysis of religious beliefs, how an individual became a Lutheran also relates to his degree of associational involvement (Table A-6). Those converted from no religious faith most frequently rank high (48 percent), and those converted from another faith (37 percent) rank high in the same proportions as those brought up in Lutheranism (37 percent). Those who became Lutheran through marriage are most likely to rank low (40 percent).

No statistically significant differences exist among the various age groups and the degree of associational involvement, but some interesting trends appear (Table A-7). The younger layman more often ranks low on the index. Among those ranking high, associational involvement progressively increases with age to a peak in the 41 to 50 age category, whereupon a declining pattern prevails. Finally, the data suggest that the longer a person's family has lived in America, the more likely he is to rank high in associational involvement. Thus, 29 percent of first generation, 31 percent of the second, and 36 percent of the third and fourth generation Americans rank high.

No meaningful differences in associational involvement occur between males and females, between white and Negro Lutherans, by nationality background, or by type of schools attended. Also, neither the type of community in which one was reared, nor the location of his church in the metropolitan area, has any significant effect on his ranking on the index.

RELIGIOUS PRACTICES

While the four Lutheran bodies do not vary greatly in associational involvement, large differences exist in the more personal religious practices. Three questions in the study measure this aspect of an individual's religiousness, each aimed at a different type of religious practice. All three relate to private practices, as contrasted to associational involvement, which takes place within the organized religious group. The first question was worded: "When you have decisions to make in your everyday life, do you ask yourself what God would want you to do?" The second question asked how often table prayers or grace at mealtime were spoken in the home, and the third asked if an individual

TABLE 2-7
Frequency of Table Prayers or Grace for Laymen,
By Branch of Lutheranism

| | By Percentage | | | |
	LCA	ALC	MS	WS
At all meals	18	33	45	42
At least once a day	32	25	27	28
At least once a week	12	9	8	6
Only on special occasions	26	22	11	18
Never or hardly ever	12	11	9	6

$p = .001$

had ever personally tried to convert a nonbeliever to his religious faith.

The percentages of laymen who often ask themselves what God would want them to do when they have decisions to make vary significantly, from 34 percent in the LCA, 39 percent in the ALC, 44 percent in the WS, to 47 percent in the MS. The differences among the four branches relating to table prayers or grace are shown in Table 2-7. Here laymen indicating that prayers are said at all meals range from a low of 18 percent in the LCA to a high of 45 percent in the MS. The third question reflects a trend similar to those in the other two. The percentages of individuals who say they have tried to convert a nonbeliever to their faith many times or a few times range from 26 percent in the LCA, 34 percent in the ALC, 44 percent in the MS, to 48 percent in the WS.

The Religious Practices Index

The Religious Practices Index was constructed in the

same manner as the other indexes.[12] Large differences exist among the four Lutheran bodies regarding religious practices (Table 2-8). The MS and WS have the largest per-

TABLE 2-8
Lay Rankings on Religious Practices Index, By Branch of Lutheranism

Branch	Low	By Percentage Moderate	High
LCA	47	31	22
ALC	36	32	32
MS	25	31	44
WS	23	33	44

$p = .05$

centages of their members ranking high, with 44 percent each, and the LCA has the lowest at 22 percent. Apparently Lutherans from the theologically more conservative branches not only are somewhat more organizationally involved, but their members also carry out more noninstitutional religious practices.

Social Correlates of Religious Practices

Females, Negroes, those who have attended parochial schools, Lutherans of German descent, and those reared in rural areas are all more likely to rank high on the Religious Practices Index. How one became a Lutheran has some bearing on his religious practices, but his ranking does not relate to his social class, length of residence in America, or the location of his church in the metropolitan area.

Lutherans generally are concentrated into two nationality groups—those from Germany and those from the Scandinavian countries. Those of German descent (43 percent) are much more likely to rank high on the index than those of Scandinavian descent (27 percent).

Thirty-nine percent of the Lutheran females and 30 percent of the males rank high, and 28 percent of the females and 40 percent of the males rank low. Fifty-nine percent of the Negro and 35 percent of the white Lutherans rank high on the index. Although these differences are statistically significant, they should be interpreted with caution, inasmuch as there were only twenty-two Negro laymen in the sample.

Forty-four percent of the laymen who have had some Lutheran parochial school education rank high, as compared to 33 percent who have attended public schools only. Although the differences are not statistically significant, Lutherans reared in large urban areas generally carry out fewer religious practices than those reared elsewhere. For example, 38 percent of those brought up in a large city, as compared to 25 percent reared on a farm, rank low on the Religious Practices Index (Table A-9). Lutherans reared on a farm (43 percent ranking high) are most likely to carry out religious practices. Again, although the differences are not statistically significant, those who became Lutherans through conversion, excluding converts at marriage, are most likely to rank high (42 percent and 38 percent) on the Religious Practices Index (Table A-10). Those who became Lutheran through marriage most likely rank low (41 percent).

RELIGIOUS KNOWLEDGE

The overall level of religious knowledge among Lutheran laymen is low—particularly in the LCA and ALC. Nine questions measured this dimension of religious commitment. The questions dealt with knowledge about the Bible and were used because Lutheranism traditionally has been a Bible-centered religion. Laymen were asked to determine whether the following two statements were from the Bible: "Blessed are the strong: for they shall be the sword of God" and "Let your women keep silence in the churches: for it is not permitted unto them to speak." Next, the laymen were asked to recite the seventh commandment. The final questions asked for the identification of the Biblical character associated with the following events in the Bible: a lion's den, a giant, a burning bush, a kiss, a fish or whale, and the disciple that denied Christ three times.[13]

The Religious Knowledge Index

On the Religious Knowledge Index individuals scored one point for each question answered correctly.[14] While the knowledge differences among the branches are not as great as with some other dimensions, they are statistically significant (Table 2-9).[15] Both the MS and WS have the largest percentages of laymen ranking high (44 percent), while the ALC has 35 percent and the LCA 25 percent. The higher levels of knowledge among MS and WS laymen probably can be attributed largely to the fact that these two branches maintain parochial schools.

TABLE 2-9
Lay Rankings on Religious Knowledge Index, By Branch of Lutheranism

Branch	Low	By Percentage Moderate	High
LCA	29	46	25
ALC	25	40	35
MS	22	34	44
WS	23	33	44

$p = .01$

Social Correlates of Religious Knowledge

An individual's ranking on the Religious Knowledge Index varies with his social class standing (Table A-11). Of the lower class, 28 percent rank high in religious knowledge, in contrast to 43 percent of the upper class Lutherans. Individuals of German descent are much more likely to rank high (45 percent) than those of Scandinavian background (28 percent) (Table A-12). Those who have attended a parochial school are much more knowledgeable than those who have attended public schools only. Fifty-three percent of the Lutherans who have some parochial school education rank high on religious knowledge, as compared to 32 percent who have attended public schools only.

Lutherans whose families immigrated more recently to America tend to have a lower level of religious knowledge than the more Americanized Lutherans. Thirty-six percent of the first generation, 29 percent of the second, 26 percent of the third, and 23 percent of those who are at least fourth generation Americans rank low on the Religious Knowledge Index. Those who are Lutherans as the result of family background more often rank high (40 percent) on the index (Table A-13). Those who have fallen away from their religion and later renewed it least often rank high (21 percent). Laymen who converted to Lutheranism from no religious faith (not at marriage) are most likely to rank low (30 percent).

No significant differences in the rankings on the Religious Knowledge Index appear on the bases of age, sex, or race. Also, neither the type of community in which an individual was reared, nor the location of his church in the metropolitan area, has any relationship to his ranking.

Communal Involvement

The final aspect of religious commitment, communal involvement, was measured by the degree of influence of an individual's subcommunity contacts, such as friends or relatives, on his attitudes and behavior. Like associational involvement, this dimension is closely tied to group influences. In contrast to the formal institutional church, which is a secondary type of group pressure, the communal forces are a personal, primary type.

The first measure of communal involvement sought to gauge the intensity of the pressures on an individual to conform to Lutheran norms. Those in the sample were asked: "If for some reason you decided to become a Catholic someday, do you think any of your friends or relatives would try to discourage you, or not?" Those answering "would try" live in a communal subculture where strong pressures reinforce traditional Lutheran teachings. Laymen who give this answer range from 49 percent in the LCA and ALC, 62 percent in the MS, to 69 percent in the WS.

The second question reveals the communal influence in a different way. While the first item measures communal pressure directed toward an individual, the second determines a person's receptivity to this type of influence. The individuals were asked: "If somebody would plan and design a community or subdivision entirely for Lutherans, do you think you would like to live there?" A yes answer indicates a desire to live with, be influenced by, and gain support from one's own religious subcommunity. Again, meaningful differences exist for the four Lutheran bodies, with the yes responses ranging from 19 percent in the LCA, 25 percent in the ALC, 29 percent in the MS, to 35 percent in the WS. This means that more than one out of every three WS members wants to live in a community made up entirely of Lutherans. The percentages of "don't know" responses are greater in the conservative bodies—9 percent in the MS and 12 percent in the WS, as compared to 6 percent in both the ALC and LCA. These responses show uncertainty, and actually only about half (53 percent) of the WS laymen definitely say they do not want to live in an all-Lutheran community.

The Communal Involvement Index

The Missouri and Wisconsin synods, noted for religious isolation, rank highest on the Communal Involvement Index, which was constructed from the previous two questions.[16] The LCA, more ecumenical and more involved in local, national, and world councils of churches, is least concerned with maintaining religious isolation or Lutheran identity. About three times more laymen in the WS than in the LCA want to preserve a Lutheran subcommunal existence, or perpetuate a religious ghetto (Table 2-10). The differences among the four Lutheran bodies are statistically significant with 9 percent in the LCA, 13 percent in the ALC, 21 percent in MS, and 26 percent in the WS ranking high.

The validity questions for this index show further that the concentration of life in a total Lutheran subcommunity may be a reality for many Lutherans.[17] Their close friends and their relatives frequently are Lutherans. From childhood, in education and in housing patterns, these people have preferred to have the Lutheran *gemeinshaft*-type community predominate in their lives.

Social Correlates of Communal Involvement

Social class, nationality, rural or urban background and

the way in which an individual became a Lutheran are the only social characteristics significantly related to communal involvement. There is a small but meaningful trend for lower class Lutherans to rank at the extremes on the Communal Involvement Index, whereas middle and upper class laymen more often rank moderate (Tables A-15). Individuals of German background are more likely to rank high and less likely to rank low in communal involvement than Lutherans of Scandinavian descent. Thirty-four percent with a Scandinavian background rank low as compared to 21 percent of German descent. Persons reared in a large city are most likely to rank low (37 percent) and those reared on a farm are least likely to rank low (23 percent) (Table A-16). Finally, individuals reared as Lutherans from childhood rank highest in communal involvement (22 percent) and those converted from another religious faith, other than converts at marriage, are most likely to rank low (51 percent) (Table A-17).

INTERCORRELATION OF DIMENSIONS OF COMMITMENT

The five dimensions of religious commitment used in the study seek to measure a variety of religious orientations, and each aspect attempts to tap a different type of religious commitment. While some degree of correlation between

TABLE 2-10
Lay Rankings on Communal Involvement Index, By Branch of Lutheranism

Branch	Low	By Percentage Moderate	High
LCA	41	50	9
ALC	38	49	13
MS	30	49	21
WS	23	51	26

$p = .001$

each of the dimensions can be expected, the correlations logically might not be extremely high. Table 2-11 shows the degrees of intercorrelation among the dimensions and demonstrates that individuals express their religiosity in different, only slightly related, ways.[18]

TABLE 2-11
Intercorrelations Among the Five Indexes of Religious Commitment

	Associational Involvement	Communal Involvement	Religious Practices	Religious Knowledge
Religious Beliefs	+.264	+.251	+.333	+.231
Associational Involvement		+.144	+.344	+.302
Communal Involvement			+.204	+.120
Religious Practices				+.297

All five indexes are positively correlated, but the degree of correlation is not large for any two indexes. The highest correlation is between associational involvement and religious practices (.334). A correlation of .333 exists between religious beliefs and religious practices, and the correlation between associational involvement and religious knowledge is .302. All other correlations are below .300, with the lowest of .120 between communal involvement and religious knowledge. This last correlation suggests that religious knowledge is much more likely to be attained through the formal institutional structure of the church (associational involvement), than through family or friendship contacts (communal involvement).

These results verify the findings of Lenski, Fukuyama, and Stark and Glock,[19] none of whom found a high degree of association between the various dimensions of religious commitment analyzed in their studies. Such findings provide further support for treating religion as a multidimensional phenomenon.

III

Religion and Politics

POLITICAL AND social conservatism are inherent in the
Lutheran ethic. The ethic's view of life regards man as
sinful by nature and regards institutions such as government as keeping man's basic corruption and selfishness in
check and thereby maintaining order. The government,
the varying social classes, the unequal distribution of
wealth, and even war are viewed as part of God's divinely
willed plan. The ethic views secular reform movements
with suspicion because of man's inherent evilness. The
religious person is one who humbly submits to the existing
social order, attempts to perpetuate the status quo, and
welcomes earthly death, which is his only true hope for
relief from the bondage of sin.

If the Lutheran ethic is a viable ideological orientation
in twentieth-century America, the religiously more committed Lutherans would be expected to most reflect the
ideology. Clergymen, because of their greater theological
knowledge and understanding, would reflect this ideology
more than laymen. Our data show that clergymen who are
theologically more conservative more often 1) identify with
the Republican party; 2) prefer Republican candidates;
3) take a conservative stand against government social
welfare; 4) oppose foreign aid; and 5) take a more "hawk-

ish" stand on war. For Lutheran laymen the higher an individual ranks on the five dimensions of religious commitment, the more likely he is to identify with the Republican party and prefer Republican candidates. These findings suggest that at least part of the Lutheran ethic continues to exist among the theologically conservative and the religiously most committed Lutherans. Furthermore, the data suggest a strong relationship between a theologically conservative stance and political and social conservatism.

PARTY AND CANDIDATE PREFERENCES

Preferences for particular political parties and candidates and identification of oneself as liberal, middle-of-the-road, or conservative were used as measures of political stance. These variables are more diverse among the clergy than the laymen and relate to an individual's religious commitment. Respondents were asked if they considered themselves Republicans or Democrats or closer to the Republican or Democratic party (Table 3-1). Slightly more than half of the laymen from each Lutheran body consider themselves Republicans or closer to the Republican party. The LCA laymen (43 percent) most frequently consider themselves nearer to the Democratic party, while the WS laymen (37 percent) least frequently prefer the Democratic party.

With the clergy significant differences appear according to Lutheran branch. All the WS clergymen say they are Republicans, or consider themselves closer to the Republican party, whereas only about half of the LCA clergymen hold this view. Forty-six percent of the LCA clergymen identify with the Democratic party. Inner-city clergymen (42 percent) much less often consider themselves Republicans than clergymen from other parts of the city (77 percent) or the suburbs (76 percent).

Table 3-2 shows the political stance of Lutherans compared with their rankings on the various indexes of religious commitment. Both laymen and clergy usually feel closer to the Republican party if they are theologically conserva-

TABLE 3-1

Lay and Clergy Political Party Preferences, By Branch of Lutheranism

	Sample	Republican or Closer to Republican	By Percentage Democrat or Closer to Democratic	Don't Know
LCA	Lay	51	43	6
	Clergy	54	46	0
ALC	Lay	52	39	9
	Clergy	76	20	4
MS	Lay	55	38	7
	Clergy	79	20	1
WS	Lay	55	37	8
	Clergy	100	0	0

Lay — p = NS
Clergy — p = .05

tive, although the differences among the laymen are not statistically significant. On the other four dimensions of religious commitment (associational involvement, communal involvement, religious knowledge, and religious practices) the higher a layman ranks on each index, the more likely he is to prefer the Republican party. The Republican party, as compared to the Democratic party, comes closest to fulfilling the Lutheran ethic's demand for maintaining the status quo.

Other social variables could possibly account for the relationships in Table 3-2. The age of a clergyman, for example, relates to his political stance. Similarly, a layman's tendency to identify with the Republican party varies with his social class. The possibility that these and other variables could explain away the relationships involving religious commitment was investigated. For almost every clergy age

TABLE 3-2

Clergy and Lay Identifications with the Republican Party, By Type and Degree of Religious Commitment

Sample	Index	Ranking	Republican or Closer to Republican (By Percentage)
Clergy	Beliefs ($p = .001$)	Low	50
		Moderate	80
		High	87
Lay	Beliefs ($p = $ NS)	Low	50
		Moderate	53
		High	56
Lay	Associational Involvement ($p = .01$)	Low	47
		Moderate	52
		High	60
Lay	Practices ($p = .05$)	Low	49
		Moderate	54
		High	57
Lay	Knowledge ($p = .01$)	Low	46
		Moderate	51
		High	60
Lay	Communal Involvement ($p = .001$)	Low	44
		Moderate	56
		High	63

level, however, political ideology still relates to religious ideology (Table A-18). When laymen identifying with the Republican party are controlled for social class, communal

TABLE 3-3
Lay and Clergy Candidate Preferences in the 1960 and 1964 Presidential Elections, By Branch of Lutheranism

| Branch | Sample | By Percentage | | | |
| | | 1960* | | 1964* | |
		Nixon	Kennedy	Goldwater	Johnson
LCA	Lay	38	62	30	69
	Clergy	54	44	28	69
ALC	Lay	42	56	30	69
	Clergy	73	27	28	70
MS	Lay	42	58	31	68
	Clergy	75	25	47	52
WS	Lay	45	54	34	62
	Clergy	94	6	80	20

Lay — $p =$ NS   Lay — $p =$ NS
Clergy — $p = .05$ Clergy — $p = .01$
*"Don't Know" responses are not shown.

involvement remains an important factor associated with political party preferences (Table A-19). Similar findings result for the associational involvement and religious practices aspects of religious commitment.

As with political party designations, candidate preferences in the 1960 and 1964 presidential elections reveal greater differences among the clergy in the Lutheran branches than among the laymen (Table 3-3). Also, in most cases clergymen more often than laymen prefer Republican candidates, and those from the theologically more conservative branches of Lutheranism choose Republican candidates more often than those from the theologically liberal branches.

TABLE 3-4

*Clergy and Lay Candidate Preferences in the 1960 and 1964 Presidential
Elections, By Type and Degree of Religious Commitment*

Sample	Index	Ranking	By Percentage Nixon (1960)	Goldwater (1964)
Clergy	Beliefs	Low	55	14
		Moderate	73	35
		High	82 ($p = .001$)	65 ($p = .001$)
Lay	Beliefs	Low	36	28
		Moderate	43	30
		High	44 ($p = .05$)	36 ($p = .05$)
Lay	Associational Involvement	Low	38	28
		Moderate	37	28
		High	49 ($p = .05$)	38 ($p = .05$)
Lay	Practices	Low	39	26
		Moderate	37	32
		High	49 ($p = .05$)	35 ($p = .05$)
Lay	Knowledge	Low	32	24
		Moderate	39	31
		High	50 ($p = .001$)	36 ($p = .01$)
Lay	Communal Involvement	Low	34	28
		Moderate	44	33
		High	48 ($p = .01$)	32 ($p = $ NS)

When an individual's candidate preferences are compared with his rankings on the five dimensions of religious commitment, there is a small but significant trend for the

TABLE 3-5
Clergy Self-Designated Political Stance, By Branch of Lutheranism

Stance	By Percentage			
	LCA	ALC	MS	WS
Conservative	7	9	33	67
Middle-of-road	48	56	49	33
Liberal	34	26	10	0
None of these	11	9	8	0

theologically more conservative laymen to have preferred Nixon and Goldwater (Table 3-4). With the clergy, on the other hand, large differences occur by theological stance. For example, in the 1964 election, 14 percent of those ranking low, 35 percent ranking moderate, and 65 percent ranking high on the Religious Beliefs Index preferred Goldwater. The theologically conservative clergy almost twice as often as the highly conservative laymen preferred Nixon and Goldwater. Generally the higher a layman ranks on any of the other four indexes of religious commitment, the more likely he is to have preferred the Republican candidates. Thus, the more an individual attends church and participates in other organizational activities, the more religious practices he performs, the more religiously knowledgeable he is, and the more highly integrated he is into the Lutheran subcommunity, the more likely he is to have preferred Republicans.

As another measure of political ideology, ministers were asked to classify themselves as politically 1) conservative; 2) middle-of-the-road; 3) liberal; or 4) none of these. Table

3-5 shows the self-designations of the clergymen according to branch of Lutheranism. Table 3-6 shows designations according to theological stance. The data indicate a definite

TABLE 3-6
Clergy Self-Designated Political Stance,
By Rankings on Religious Beliefs Index

Stance	Low	By Percentage Moderate	High
Conservative	5	9	50
Middle-of-road	36	67	45
Liberal	44	15	2
None of these	15	9	3

relationship between theology and political ideology. For example, 67 percent of the WS clergy consider themselves politically conservative, compared to only 7 percent of the LCA and 9 percent of the ALC clergy. Also, 50 percent of those classified as theological conservatives call themselves political conservatives, and only 2 percent say they are political liberals. Interestingly, 15 percent of the theologically liberal clergymen could not fit themselves into one of these categories, with most referring to themselves as political radicals.

The association between conservative theology and conservative political attitudes coincides with findings of previous research.[20] However, these studies usually have confined their religious categories to Protestants, Catholics, and Jews. Johnson and Hadden have carried out more penetrating studies of the relationship between religion and political preference.[21] In studies of laymen and clergy Johnson ignored denominational lines and grouped respondents on the basis of liberal and conservative theological categories.

He found that "theological conservatism is positively associated with Republican party preference and that theological liberalism is positively associated with Democratic party preference.[22]

In Hadden's research clergymen in a national random sample categorized themselves as one of four theological types: fundamentalist, conservative, neo-orthodox, or liberal. This study of ministers from six Protestant denominations reveals that "fundamentalists and conservatives are much more likely to identify with the Republican party than neo-orthodox or liberals.[23]

SOCIAL WELFARE

The Lutheran ethic suggests a divinely willed unequal distribution of wealth. Being poor or uneducated is no disgrace, because life in the next world remains the primary concern. If such views exist today, one would expect them to be most visible among the theologically conservative clergy. It thus becomes understandable that these clergymen are not highly motivated to change the existing social order through government social welfare. In contrast, one of the goals of the theologically liberal clergy involves the reforming of this world, and social welfare appears to them to be one of the most direct means.

Four questions were used to measure Lutheran attitudes toward government action in social welfare (Table 3-7). Although statistically significant differences do not exist among the laymen of the four Lutheran bodies, meaningful variances appear among the clergy, with the LCA clergymen the most liberal and the WS clergymen the most conservative. As an example, 64 percent of the LCA clergy, as compared to none of the WS clergy, believe the government is not doing enough in such areas as housing, education, and unemployment.

TABLE 3-7
Lay and Clergy Attitudes on Social Welfare, By Branch of Lutheranism

	Sample	LCA	By Percentage ALC	MS	WS
The federal government ought to help provide medical care for all age groups. (Agreeing)	Lay ($p=$ NS)	47	42	44	41
	Clergy ($p=.05$)	56	30	31	33
I would be willing to pay more taxes so that low income families could get low-rent public housing. (Agreeing)	Lay ($p=$ NS)	41	42	33	37
	Clergy ($p=.001$)	87	69	61	33
The government is providing too many services that should be left to private enterprise. (Disagreeing)	Lay ($p=$ NS)	32	34	29	30
	Clergy ($p=.01$)	54	39	23	7
In connection with problems such as housing, unemployment, education and so on, would you say that on the whole what the government is doing is too much, about the right amount, or not enough? (Not Enough)	Lay ($p=$ NS)	31	33	29	25
	Clergy ($p=.001$)	64	42	28	0

The Social Welfare Index

The questions in Table 3-7 were used to develop the Social Welfare Index, and a high ranking indicates attitudes most favorable toward welfare programs (Table 3-8).[24] In the lay sample only extremely small differences appear among the four Lutheran bodies. With the clergy, however, marked differences exist. Clergymen from the theologically more liberal Lutheran bodies are much more

TABLE 3-8
*Lay and Clergy Rankings on the Social Welfare Index,
By Branch of Lutheranism*

Sample	Branch	Low	By Percentage Moderate	High
Lay (*p* = NS)	LCA	33	30	37
	ALC	28	33	39
	MS	32	29	39
	WS	38	25	37
Clergy (*p* = .001)	LCA	11	19	70
	ALC	24	26	50
	MS	43	27	30
	WS	54	33	13

favorable toward welfare than those from the conservative bodies, with the percentages ranking high on the index ranging from 13 percent in the WS to 70 percent in the LCA.

When the laymen's rankings on the five indexes of religious commitment are compared with their rankings on the Social Welfare Index (Table A-21), no significant differences appear except in terms of religious knowledge. The less knowledgeable the layman, the more liberal are his views on welfare. The results suggest that a conservative social philosophy may emanate from Biblical knowledge. Nevertheless, since four of the five indexes of religious commitment are unrelated to the rankings on the Social Welfare Index, the impact of religion on lay attitudes toward social welfare seems slight.

Such is not the case with the clergy, however. Clergymen

with liberal theological beliefs are much more likely to take a liberal stand regarding social welfare. Eleven percent of the clergymen ranking low, 23 percent ranking moderate, and 66 percent ranking high (most liberal) on the Social Welfare Index rank low on the Religious Beliefs Index. The same trend remains when the data are controlled for age and the social class of the ministers' parish, suggesting that social conservativism and conservative Lutheran ideol-
ᴠ relate.

ᴧutheran females tend to be slightly more liberal on ɷcial welfare questions than males. Forty-one percent of females and 32 percent of the males rank high on the ᴧ Welfare Index. Negro Lutherans are much more ɛral than whites on social welfare issues with 68 percent ɔf the Negroes ranking high on the index, compared to only 37 percent of the whites. Finally, lower class Lutherans (47 percent) more than twice as often as upper class Lutherans (23 percent) express favorable attitudes toward welfare.

FOREIGN AID AND WAR

Among the clergy theological conservatism or liberalism seems associated with an individual's attitudes on these two issues. Lutherans were asked to give agree-disagree responses to the statement: "We are spending too much to help other countries, and we shouldn't spend any money abroad except when we have to in the interest of national defense." No significant differences are found among laymen of the four Lutheran bodies, with about 50 percent of each group agreeing with the statement. Among the clergy very significant differences exist between the branches of Lutheranism. The percentages opposing foreign aid range from 13 percent in the LCA, 19 percent in the ALC, 37 percent in the MS, to a high of 40 percent in the WS. The largest gaps between lay and clergy attitudes are in the LCA and ALC.[6]

Table 3-9 compares these answers with each of the dimensions of religious commitment. No significant differences appear for laymen in terms of beliefs or communal involvement. Meaningful differences are found in connection with the Associational Involvement, Religious Practices, and Religious Knowledge indexes. In each of these cases the higher a respondent ranks, the less likely he is to take a conservative stand on foreign aid. With the clergy, a conservative stand on foreign aid increases with the level of theological conservatism. Eight percent of the clergy ranking low, 27 percent ranking moderate, and 44 percent ranking high on the Religious Beliefs Index take a conservative stand on foreign aid. For the clergy conservative theology appears to relate to conservative attitudes on foreign aid. In contrast, for the laymen increased religiousness in terms of associational involvement, religious practices, and religious knowledge results in more liberal attitudes on foreign aid. Here humanitarian concerns not related to traditional Lutheran theological beliefs apparently are involved.

On questions about war only small differences exist among the laymen of the four Lutheran bodies, whereas the clergy show significant variations (Table 3-10). Thus, the attitudes of the WS clergy parallel most closely those of the laymen. The Lutherans were asked to react to the two statements "We should have sent troops to Çuba before Castro became so powerful" and "We should start bombing North Vietnam with everything we have and get this war over with."

When these questions are compared to type of religious commitment, few significant differences exist between one's attitudes toward war and his rankings on the indexes of religious commitment (Table A-22). Meaningful differences among the clergy, however, appear when theological stance is taken into account, with the theologically more

TABLE 3-9

Clergy and Lay Attitudes on Foreign Aid, By Type and Degree of Religious Commitment

Sample	Index	Ranking	Conservative Stance (By Percentage)
Clergy	Beliefs ($p = .001$)	Low	8
		Moderate	27
		High	44
Lay	Beliefs ($p = $ NS)	Low	53
		Moderate	55
		High	47
Lay	Associational Involvement ($p = .05$)	Low	58
		Moderate	50
		High	47
Lay	Communal Involvement ($p = $ NS)	Low	54
		Moderate	49
		High	56
Lay	Practices ($p = .01$)	Low	78
		Moderate	53
		High	45
Lay	Knowledge ($p = .001$)	Low	66
		Moderate	49
		High	45

conservative clergymen being more hawkish on both questions.[6] Thirty-eight percent of the clergy ranking high on the Religious Beliefs Index think "we should have sent

TABLE 3-10
Lay and Clergy Attitudes on War, By Branch of Lutheranism

	Sample	LCA	By Percentage ALC	MS	WS
We should have sent troops to Cuba before Castro became so powerful. (Agreeing)	Lay ($p =$ NS)	42	45	48	47
	Clergy ($p = .001$)	21	22	34	47
We should start bombing North Viet Nam with everything we have and get this war over with. (Agreeing)	Lay ($p =$ NS)	36	36	42	37
	Clergy ($p = .001$)	9	17	28	43

troops to Cuba" and 38 percent think that "we should bomb North Vietnam with everything we have." Persons agreeing with the last statement apparently are sanctioning even the use of atomic bombs in the Vietnam war.

The theologically conservative clergymen's attitudes on war are not easily explained. The Lutheran ethic recognizes 'just" wars and, therefore, an individual could define the Vietnam war and a Cuban war as justifiable. Also, since the ethic regards life in this world as less important than life in the next, death as a result of war does not necessarily constitute a tragedy. The threat of atheistic Communism may also lead to the more prowar attitudes among the conservative clergymen.

The attitudes of the most conservative clergymen are very similar to the averages of all laymen. The greatest differences exist between the anti-war attitudes of the moderately conservative and theologically liberal clergymen, and the prowar attitudes of most laymen.

The differences expressed among the clergy may indicate a movement by theologically liberal clergymen away from conservative Lutheran theology and toward a more humanitarian emphasis. Indeed, among theologically liberal clergymen an ethic of love toward fellow human beings in this world may be replacing the Lutheran ethic's emphasis on saving souls for the next world.

IV

Religion, Civil Rights, and Civil Liberties

IN LUTHER'S TIME a fixed class system based upon a patriarchal-agrarian medieval social hierarchy prevailed. To Luther this was the ideal social system and the one which offered the best possibilities of living a God-pleasing life. Serfdom and slavery were seen as the very foundation of society. Thus, as the Lutheran ethic developed, it stressed the spiritual equality of man in the eyes of God, but it also suggested that divinely willed temporal inequalities exist. Presumably, the inequalities exist for races as well as for social classes.

The Lutheran doctrine of the calling also is paramount in this connection. The Lutheran ethic regards all callings as spiritually equal, and whether one is master or slave, the recommended pattern of life consists of abiding by and enduring one's call and trusting in God. The doctrine implies that the existing order on earth at any particular time or place is God's will. To attempt to change that order by human means, such as through social revolution, is contrary to the ethic's ideal pattern of behavior.

Finally, developing out of the Lutheran ethic is a belief that Lutheranism is the one "true" religion. Lutheran ideology quite naturally supports intolerance, suspicion, and distrust of Jews, Roman Catholics, and atheists.

In this study, consistent with the Lutheran ethic, the theologically more conservative clergymen express attitudes suggesting 1) greater prejudice toward Negroes; 2) a higher degree of anti-Semitism; 3) greater concern about Catholic power in this country; and 4) strong distrust of atheists. On these questions the laymen are generally more intolerant than the clergy, although in many cases their attitudes are comparable to the WS clergy's attitudes. The largest gulf between the laymen and clergy is between the theologically liberal clergy and the majority of the laymen.

Theologically conservative clergymen strongly resist the granting of particular civil liberties. These findings are consistent with the Lutheran ethic model, which prescribes a distrust of man and an emphasis on government controls deemed necessary to restrain man's sinfulness.

ATTITUDES TOWARD NEGROES

According to the Gallup Poll, Lutheranism has a lower percentage of nonwhite members than any other major Christian denomination in the United States.[1] Since Lutheranism has only one percent nonwhite members, the question of whether anti-Negro feeling exists among Lutherans is relevant. Table 4-1 shows five questions designed to measure the attitudes of white Lutherans toward Negroes.

Laymen show considerable anti-Negro feeling, but no significant differences are found among the four Lutheran branches.[2] The clergymen, on the other hand, less often express anti-Negro attitudes, but there is considerable variation among the Lutheran branches. For example, on the statement "Negroes could solve many of their own problems if they would not be so irresponsible and carefree about life" the percentages of clergymen agreeing range from a

TABLE 4-1

Lay and Clergy Attitudes Toward Negroes, By Branch of Lutheranism

	Sample		By Percentage		
		LCA	ALC	MS	WS
In general Negroes cannot be trusted. (Agreeing)	Lay (*p* = NS)	20	22	20	23
	Clergy (*p* = NS)	0	4	6	7
Negroes could solve many of their own problems if they would not be so irresponsible and carefree about life. (Agreeing)	Lay (*p* = NS)	74	73	78	70
	Clergy (*p* = .01)	19	17	38	64
I basically disapprove of the Negro civil rights movement in America. (Agreeing)	Lay (*p* = NS)	47	49	41	49
	Clergy (*p* = .01)	11	4	20	39
Would you be at all disturbed or unhappy if a Negro with the same income and education as you moved into your block? (Yes)	Lay (*p* = NS)	40	41	42	32
	Clergy (*p* = NS)	2	0	4	7
Personally, do you think white students and Negro students should go to the same schools? (Separate or Don't Know)	Lay (*p* = NS)	25	21	22	24
	Clergy (*p* = NS)	0	4	5	13

low of 17 percent in the ALC to a high of 64 percent in the WS. Regarding the statement "I basically disapprove of the Negro civil rights movement in America" only 4 percent

TABLE 4-2
Lay and Clergy Rankings on the Race Prejudice Index,
By Branch of Lutheranism

Sample	Branch	Low	*By Percentage* Moderate	High
Lay ($p =$ NS)	LCA	15	51	34
	ALC	15	51	34
	MS	13	55	32
	WS	17	51	32
Clergy ($p = .05$)	LCA	76	24	0
	ALC	76	22	2
	MS	57	35	8
	WS	28	65	7

of the ALC clergy agree, compared to 39 percent in the WS. On the other three questions the clergy from the theologically more conservative Lutheran bodies have slightly higher percentages of anti-Negro responses, but the differences are not statistically significant.

The Race Prejudice Index

On the Race Prejudice Index[3] no meaningful differences appear among the laymen of the four Lutheran bodies (Table 4-2). With the clergy, however, significant differences occur. Clergymen ranking low on the index (least prejudiced) range from 76 percent in both the LCA and

ALC, 56 percent in the MS, to 29 percent in the WS. While differences between the branches of Lutheranism are much greater for clergymen than laymen, laymen show considerably higher levels of prejudice. In each Lutheran body one-third of the laymen rank high and more than 50 percent rank moderate on the index.

Table 4-3 compares the five indexes of religious commitment with an individual's ranking on the Race Prejudice Index. A layman's ranking on the Religious Beliefs Index and his views regarding Negroes do not relate. However, the higher one ranks on the Associational Involvement, Religious Practices, and Religious Knowledge indexes, the less apt he is to hold prejudiced attitudes toward Negroes. In relation to communal involvement, however, the opposite pattern prevails. Here the higher an individual ranks on the Communal Involvement Index, the greater the degree of race prejudice. The findings suggest that race prejudice is fostered and supported within one's primary group relationships—that is, by his close friends, family, and relatives.

While theological stance of laymen has no bearing on race prejudice, a strong relationship exists for the clergy. The theologically more liberal clergymen show a low level of prejudice, and the theologically more conservative clergymen more often rank high or moderate on the Race Prejudice Index. Of clergymen ranking low (liberal) on the index 92 percent rank low, 6 percent moderate, and 2 percent high on the prejudice index, suggesting an inverse relationship between liberal theology and racial prejudice.

The Lutheran ethic seems very important in explaining the findings. Conceivably one reason for the greater prejudice among theologically conservative clergymen may be their tendency to be Biblical literalists, and particular sections of the Old Testament often have been interpreted as supporting racial segregation. Those most prejudiced are also likely to believe that divinely willed earthly inequalities do exist. The laymen illustrate this dramatically, and almost nine out of ten laymen rank high on the Race Prej-

TABLE 4-3
Clergy and Lay Rankings on Race Prejudice Index,
By Type and Degree of Religious Commitment

Sample	Index	Ranking	Low	By Percentage Moderate	High
Clergy	Beliefs ($p = .001$)	Low	92	6	2
		Moderate	62	35	3
		High	44	47	9
Lay	Beliefs ($p =$ NS)	Low	16	51	33
		Moderate	15	50	35
		High	15	54	31
Lay	Associational Involvement ($p = .001$)	Low	10	47	43
		Moderate	17	49	34
		High	18	59	23
Lay	Communal Involvement ($p = .001$)	Low	20	53	27
		Moderate	14	52	34
		High	7	50	43
Lay	Practices ($p = .05$)	Low	13	50	37
		Moderate	15	49	36
		High	17	56	27
Lay	Knowledge ($p = .001$)	Low	4	44	52
		Moderate	16	51	33
		High	22	58	20

udice Index, agreeing that "while men are spiritually equal
in God's eyes, there are in fact basic differences in intelli-
gence among the races." The majority of the theologically

TABLE 4-4
Clergy Rankings on the Race Prejudice Index, By Age

Age	Low	By Percentage Moderate	High
30 and under	97	3	0
31-40	71	28	1
41-50	61	34	5
51-60	51	41	8
61 and over	26	53	21

$p = .01$

conservative laymen also see the separation of men into
classes and groups as the direct result of God's will and thus
as something not to be tampered with (Table A-23).

For the clergy, race prejudice varies as greatly with age as
with theological stance. Table 4-4 shows that younger clergymen more often than older clergymen rank low on the
Race Prejudice Index. With age held constant, however,
the relationship between conservative theology and race
prejudice still exists. A layman's ranking on the Race Prejudice Index varies with his social class standing (Table
4-5). The differences here approximate those found in the
comparisons of race prejudice and both associational involvement and religious knowledge. However, when social
class is held constant, the relationships found among the
various dimensions of religious commitment and race prejudice still exist. These findings support Lenski's conclusions
that religion is a variable comparable in importance to social class.[4]

ATTITUDES TOWARD JEWS

Glock and Stark suggest in *Christian Beliefs and Anti-Semitism* that the Christian religion as practiced in certain denominations may actually perpetuate anti-Semitic

TABLE 4-5
Lay Rankings on the Race Prejudice Index, By Social Class

Class	Low	By Percentage Moderate	High
Lower	10	48	42
Middle	16	53	31
Upper	23	57	20

$p = .001$

feelings. They suggest that individuals from conservative Protestant bodies more often have anti-Semitic attitudes than those from liberal denominations. To investigate these propositions further the attitudes of Lutherans toward Jews were measured by three questions (Table 4-6). More than 40 percent of the laymen think Jews are less fair than Protestants in their business dealings. With the clergy significant differences appear among the four Lutheran bodies, although the overall percentages are much smaller than for the laymen. The clergy responses range from 11 percent in the LCA to 27 percent in the MS. Another 20 percent of the WS clergy (4 percent in the MS and LCA, 2 percent in the ALC) say they are uncertain or didn't know whether Jews are less fair, which may reveal a reluctance to answer a question obviously measuring negative attitudes toward Jews. However, it could also mean that a significant minority of the WS clergy live in relatively isolated subcommunities and thus have never had much contact with Jews.

Only about half as many laymen express concern about Jews' trying to get too much power, as compared with those who think Jews are less fair in business. Laymen answering yes on the power question range from 19 percent in the ALC to 25 percent in the MS. Among the clergy 9 percent in the ALC, 12 percent in the LCA, 31 percent in the MS, and 47 percent in the WS give affirmative responses. Obvious differences arise among the clergy from the liberal and conservative branches of Lutheranism regarding Jewish power in the United States.

Agreement with the statement "I tend to distrust a person who does not believe in Jesus" would suggest distrust of Jews, the largest non-Christian minority in the United States. For laymen, the percentages agreeing range from 37 percent in the ALC to 46 percent in the WS. The clergymen less often agree, with the exception of the WS. Clergymen agreeing range from 13 percent in the ALC, 20 percent in the LCA, 26 percent in the MS, to 44 percent in the WS.

The Anti-Semitism Index

The percentage of WS clergymen ranking high (most prejudiced) on the Anti-Semitism Index closely approximates the lay rankings in each Lutheran branch (Table 4-7). Approximately one-third of the laymen fall into each of the categories of low, moderate, and high on the Anti-Semitism Index,[5] with no meaningful differences among the branches. The clergymen, though, show statistically significant differences. For example, those ranking most prejudiced (high) range from 8 percent in the ALC to 31 percent in the WS.

Among the clergy a strong relationship between theological stance and ranking on the Anti-Semitism index appears (Table 4-8). Theologically liberal clergymen considerably

TABLE 4-6

Lay and Clergy Attitudes Toward Jews, By Branch of Lutheranism

			By Percentage		
	Sample	LCA	ALC	MS	WS
Jews are *less fair* than Protestants in their business dealings. (Agreeing)	Lay (p = NS)	40	37	43	44
	Clergy (p = .05)	11	15	27	20
Jewish people have been trying to get too much power in this country. (Agreeing)	Lay (p = NS)	24	19	25	22
	Clergy (p = .01)	12	9	31	47
"I tend to distrust a person who does not believe in Jesus." (Agreeing)	Lay (p = NS)	38	37	43	46
	Clergy (p = .01)	20	13	26	44

TABLE 4-7

Lay and Clergy Rankings on the Anti-Semitism Index, By Branch of Lutheranism

			By Percentage	
Sample	Branch	Low	Moderate	High
Lay (p = NS)	LCA	36	31	33
	ALC	43	27	30
	MS	30	38	32
	WS	33	31	36
Clergy (p = .05)	LCA	68	22	10
	ALC	73	19	8
	MS	49	25	26
	WS	46	23	31

less often express anti-Semitic attitudes than the theologically more conservative. Of the clergymen ranking low on the Religious Beliefs Index 81 percent rank low, 17 percent rank moderate, and 2 percent rank high on anti-Semitism. Although less dramatic, a similar trend appears for laymen.

Significant differences also result when associational and communal involvement are compared with a layman's ranking on the Anti-Semitism Index. The higher he ranks in communal involvement, the more likely he is to be anti-Semitic. The exact opposite trend seems true for associational involvement. In this case the higher a layman ranks on the Associational Involvement Index, the less anti-Semitic he is.

Earlier studies also have shown race prejudice to be lower among individuals who are more associationally involved and higher among those who are communally involved. Apparently the religious subcommunity perpetuates the greatest intolerance, and not the associational aspect of church involvement as is sometimes charged. In fact, associational activity appears to correspond with a decrease in prejudiced attitudes. These findings strongly support the conclusions of Lenski in his study of Detroit-area Protestants, Catholics, and Jews and reemphasize the importance of differentiating between the communal and associational dimensions of religious commitment.[6]

The Religious Sources of Anti-Semitism

Four questions were devised to test the possibility that anti-Semitic attitudes emanate from religious sources (Table 4-9). Results similar to Glock and Stark's appear,[7] and meaningful differences do exist among the four Lutheran branches for both laymen and clergy (Table 4-9). In every case members of the theologically more conservative branches (MS and WS) agree more often with the statements. The differences among laymen and clergy in each branch parallel the differences found in connection

TABLE 4-8
Clergy and Lay Rankings on the Anti-Semitism Index,
By Type and Degree of Religious Commitment

Sample	Index	Ranking	Low	By Percentage Moderate	High
Clergy	Beliefs ($p = .001$)	Low	81	17	2
		Moderate	59	22	19
		High	44	28	28
Lay	Beliefs ($p = .01$)	Low	43	32	25
		Moderate	37	31	32
		High	27	35	38
Lay	Associational Involvement ($p = .05$)	Low	32	30	38
		Moderate	34	35	31
		High	39	32	29
Lay	Communal Involvement ($p = .001$)	Low	47	29	24
		Moderate	32	33	35
		High	21	37	42
Lay	Practices ($p = NS$)	Low	41	29	30
		Moderate	32	33	35
		High	32	35	33
Lay	Knowledge ($p = NS$)	Low	34	30	36
		Moderate	34	32	34
		High	37	34	29

with religious beliefs. The clergymen in the MS and WS are more conservative, whereas the LCA and ALC clergy are more liberal in relation to their laymen.

TABLE 4-9

Lay and Clergy Responses to Religious Sources of Anti-Semitism Questions, By Branch of Lutheranism

| | Sample | By Percentage | | | |
		LCA	ALC	MS	WS
The Jews can never be forgiven for what they did to Jesus until they accept Him as the true Savior. (Agreeing)	Lay ($p = .001$)	37	40	53	66
	Clergy ($p = .001$)	26	28	60	86
The curse which the Jews called down upon themselves after crucifying Jesus still rests on them and their children to this very day. (Agreeing)	Lay ($p = .001$)	34	37	51	56
	Clergy ($p = .001$)	19	28	55	81
The reason the Jews have so much trouble is because God is punishing them for rejecting Jesus. (Agreeing)	Lay ($p = .001$)	16	19	26	30
	Clergy ($p = .001$)	8	7	36	56
Today God is using individuals and nations to carry out his continuing punishment against the Jews. (Agreeing)	Lay ($p = .01$)	5	7	13	17
	Clergy ($p = .001$)	0	7	23	56

The rankings on the Religious Sources of Anti-Semitism Index (Table 4-10) show meaningful differences among the four bodies for both laymen and clergy.[8] The theologically more conservative the branch of Lutheranism, the more frequently its members and clergy rank moderate or high on the index.

The higher an individual ranks on every index of religious commitment, the more likely he is to rank high on the Religious Sources of Anti-Semitism Index (Table 4-11). Only for associational involvement are the differences not statistically significant, but a trend similar to those in

TABLE 4-10
Lay and Clergy Rankings on the Religious Sources of Anti-Semitism Index,
By Branch of Lutheranism

Sample	Branch	Low	By Percentage Moderate	High
Lay	LCA	49	38	13
	ALC	46	42	12
	MS	28	52	20
	WS	22	52	26
				$p = .001$
Clergy	LCA	69	26	5
	ALC	60	32	8
	MS	27	42	31
	WS	6	47	47
				$p = .001$

the other indexes appears. Possibly church services and other institutional activities emphasize values of equality and nondiscrimination, thus offsetting other types of influence and neutralizing anti-Semitism among the more associationally involved. The religious beliefs of Lutheran clergymen show an especially dramatic relationship with the Religious Sources of Anti-Semitism Index. Of those clergy ranking low on the Religious Beliefs Index, 85 percent rank low, 14 percent moderate, and one percent high on the Religious Sources of Anti-Semitism Index.

To demonstrate that anti-Semitic attitudes can be partially accounted for by religious ideology one must show that an individual's ranking on the Religious Sources of Anti-Semitism Index relates to his ranking on the Anti-Semitism Index. A strong relationship exists between a person's rankings on two indexes (Table 4-12). High-ranking persons on the Religious Sources of Anti-Semitism Index more frequently express anti-Semitic attitudes, and those ranking low less often do, particularly the clergy.

TABLE 4-11
Clergy and Lay Rankings on the Religious Sources of Anti-Semitism Index, By Rankings on the Indexes of Religious Commitment

Sample	Index	Ranking	Low	By Percentage Moderate	High
Clergy	Beliefs ($p = .001$)	Low	85	14	1
		Moderate	46	39	15
		High	11	52	37
Lay	Beliefs ($p = .001$)	Low	59	33	8
		Moderate	37	47	16
		High	17	55	28
Lay	Associational Involvement ($p = $ NS)	Low	42	42	16
		Moderate	34	49	17
		High	32	47	21
Lay	Communal Involvement ($p = .001$)	Low	48	39	13
		Moderate	34	49	17
		High	19	53	28
Lay	Practices ($p = .01$)	Low	48	41	11
		Moderate	37	46	17
		High	24	52	24
Lay	Knowledge ($p = .05$)	Low	39	47	14
		Moderate	38	48	14
		High	31	44	25

According to traditional Lutheran theology Jews are "damned," and there is no hope for these "lost people" unless they convert to Christianity. The attitudes of Lu-

TABLE 4-12

Lay and Clergy Rankings on the Anti-Semitic Index,
By Rankings on the Religious Sources of Anti-Semitism Index

Sample	Religious Sources Ranking	By Percentage		
		Low	Moderate	High
Lay	Low	49	33	25
($p = .001$)	Moderate	43	48	48
	High	9	19	27
Clergy	Low	63	28	2
($p = .001$)	Moderate	29	52	39
	High	9	20	59

therans toward Jews and the Lutheran ethic (particularly as it relates to the separation of the two kingdoms and government noninterference) likely contributed to the conditions in Nazi Germany which resulted in the genocidal treatment of Jews. Martin Luther's feelings toward Jews were not consistent, and in his later life he recommended harsh treatment for them. Luther thought that God had stricken the Jews with madness and, therefore, radical measures were in order. He thus recommended destruction of synagogues and prayer books, prohibition of rabbis' teaching, confiscation of wealth, and banishment from the country.[9]

ATTITUDES TOWARD CATHOLICS

Lutheran laymen and clergy think Roman Catholics are fairer in business dealings than they think Jews to be, but Lutherans are considerably more concerned about Catholic than Jewish power in America. The two questions asked about Jews were asked also about Catholics (Table 4-13). Only a small percentage of the laymen and clergy think

TABLE 4-13
Lay and Clergy Attitudes Toward Catholics, By Branch of Lutheranism

Question	Sample	By Percentage			
		LCA	ALC	MS	WS
Catholics are *less fair* in their business dealings. (Agreeing)	Lay (p = NS)	8	10	9	12
	Clergy (p = .05)	4	0	9	13
Do you feel that Catholics have been trying to get too much power in this country? (Yes)	Lay (p = .05)	29	28	29	37
	Clergy (p = .001)	21	22	45	80

Catholics are less fair than Protestants in their business dealings, with only minor differences among the four Lutheran bodies. Clergymen calling Catholics less fair range from none in the ALC to 13 in the WS.

Those who see Catholics as trying to get too much power range from 28 percent in the ALC to 37 percent in the WS for laymen and from 21 percent in the LCA to 80 percent in the WS for clergy. Obviously, the greatest apprehension about Catholic power in America exists among clergy from theologically conservative branches (MS and WS).

The major relationship between a laymen's view of Catholics and his rank on the various dimensions of religious commitment occurs with communal involvement (Table A-24). Laymen who see Catholics as less fair in business range from 6 percent of those ranking low, 10 percent ranking moderate, to 18 percent ranking high on the Communal Involvement Index. Similarly, those who think Catholics have been trying to get too much power range from 22 percent ranking low, 33 percent ranking moderate, to 39 percent ranking high in communal involvement. The data suggest that anti-Catholic attitudes do not evolve from, nor are in any way significantly affected by, a layman's religious beliefs, knowledge, practices, or associational involvement. The theologically more conservative clergymen show considerable concern about Catholic power. On this question 14 percent ranking low, 26 ranking moderate, and 60 percent ranking high on the Religious Beliefs Index believe that Catholics are trying to get too much power (Table A-49).

ATTITUDES TOWARD NONBELIEVERS

Lutheran clergymen are much more tolerant than laymen in their opinions about individuals who do not believe in God. The respondents were asked to agree or disagree with the statement "A person who says that there is no God is likely to hold dangerous political ideas." Laymen agreeing range from 60 percent in the LCA, 63 percent in the ALC, 67 percent in the WS, to 70 percent in the MS. In contrast, fewer clergy in all four groups agree, ranging from 17 percent in the LCA, 19 percent in the ALC, 47 percent in the MS, to 56 percent in the WS. Thus, Lutheran clergymen tend to be much more tolerant than laymen in evaluating nonbelievers. Only the WS clergy approach the attitudes of the laymen, indicating a distrust of nonbelievers.

An individual's theological stance appears to influence his feelings about atheists. Significant differences show up among laymen and clergy according to their rankings on the Religious Beliefs Index, and for the laymen on the Communal Involvement and Religious Practices indexes (Table A-25). The theologically more conservative an individual, the more religious practices he performs, and the greater his integration into the Lutheran subcommunity, the more he thinks nonbelievers are apt to be politically dangerous.

TABLE 4-14
Lay and Clergy Attitudes on Civil Liberties, By Branch of Lutheranism

		By Percentage			
	Sample	LCA	ALC	MS	WS
The right of free speech includes the right for someone to make speeches in favor of Communism or a dictatorship. (Agreeing)	Lay (*p* = NS)	48	54	43	47
	Clergy (*p* = .001)	76	78	53	47
Publications that dwell on sex and use obscene language should be banned from the newsstand. (Disagreeing)	Lay (*p* = NS)	11	9	9	6
	Clergy (*p* = .001)	52	37	22	6
Do you feel that books which are strongly and unfairly biased against your religious group ought to be allowed to be sold in bookstores? (Yes)	Lay (*p* = NS)	66	73	68	69
	Clergy (*p* = NS)	94	93	80	93

CIVIL LIBERTIES

Theologically conservative clergymen closely parallel the laymen of all Lutheran branches in opposing certain civil liberties. Three questions were used, each designed to measure a slightly different facet of the civil liberties issue (Table 4-14).

Approximately half the laymen from each of the branches think that "the right of free speech includes the right for someone to make speeches in favor of Communism or a dictatorship" (Table 4-14), with no major differences among the four groups. Larger differences are evident among the clergy, however, with a high of 78 percent in the ALC and a low of 47 percent in the WS agreeing with the

TABLE 4-15
*Lay and Clergy Rankings on the Civil Liberties Index,
By Branch of Lutheranism*

Sample	Branch	Low	By Percentage Moderate	High
Lay (*p* = NS)	LCA	21	35	44
	ALC	17	34	49
	MS	18	42	40
	WS	18	41	41
Clergy (*p* = .001)	LCA	1	19	80
	ALC	2	19	79
	MS	13	33	54
	WS	7	40	53

statement. All but a few of the laymen feel that obscene publications should be banned from the newsstand. While there are only small differences among the four lay branches, very significant differences occur among the clergy. More than half the LCA clergy, but only 6 percent of the WS clergy, oppose banning of publications. The percentage of WS clergymen disagreeing is exactly the same as the WS lay percentage and quite close to the lay percentages in the other groups also. On the question about biased books, although there are no significant differences among the four Lutheran branches for either laymen or clergy approximately 70 percent of the laymen believe that books

which strongly or unfairly bias their religious group should
be allowed to be sold. Clergymen are even more liberal,
with nine out of ten giving an affirmative response.

TABLE 4-16
*Clergy and Lay Rankings on the Civil Liberties Index,
By Type and Degree of Religious Commitment*

Sample	Index	Ranking	By Percentage		
			Low	Moderate	High
Clergy	Beliefs $(p = .001)$	Low	0	9	91
		Moderate	4	26	70
		High	14	42	44
Lay	Beliefs $(p = .01)$	Low	13	34	53
		Moderate	18	40	42
		High	22	40	38
Lay	Associational Involvement $(p = NS)$	Low	19	36	45
		Moderate	17	44	39
		High	19	35	46
Lay	Communal Involvement $(p = .01)$	Low	18	34	48
		Moderate	16	42	42
		High	26	39	35
Lay	Practices $(p = NS)$	Low	18	35	47
		Moderate	18	40	42
		High	19	40	41
Lay	Knowledge $(p = .001)$	Low	28	40	32
		Moderate	16	41	43
		High	13	36	51

The Civil Liberties Index

On the Civil Liberties Index[10] the laymen of the four groups show small differences in their rankings (Table 4-15). For the clergy, however, meaningful variances appear, and in all four bodies the clergy are more liberal than the laymen in granting civil liberties.

A layman's ranking on the Religious Beliefs, Communal Involvement, and Religious Knowledge indexes varies significantly with his stand on civil liberties (Table 4-16). The higher one ranks in terms of religious beliefs and communal involvement, the less tolerant he is on civil liberties. On the other hand, in the case of religious knowledge, the more knowledgeable the individual, the more liberal he is regarding civil liberties. The data show no relationship for associational involvement, making the present study contrary to the research of Stouffer, who found church attenders more intolerant than nonattenders on questions of civil liberties.[11] Finally, theologically conservative clergymen less frequently rank high on the Civil Liberties Index (44 percent) than liberal clergymen (91 percent).

V

Religion and Morality

FOR LUTHER the Ten Commandments served as an ideal (although unobtainable) moral standard and as a stimulus for repentance by pointing out man's sinful nature and helplessness. Today the Law not only plays an important part in Lutheran ideology, but it overwhelmingly dominates the thinking of most laymen. For example, in complete contradiction to traditional Lutheran theology emphasizing the grace of God, the majority of laymen interviewed think that they can achieve salvation by keeping the Ten Commandments. These Lutherans obtain their moral norms from Old Testament Law. Most laymen and theologically conservative clergy regard only items specifically mentioned in the Bible as moral problems. They do not recognize newer moral issues and do not broaden Biblical proscriptions to include modern versions of older moral precepts. An example is the issue of smoking. Despite substantial evidence that smoking is a means of committing suicide, the attitudes of Lutherans on the question in no way relate to their religious commitment. Sexual behavior is by far the most important moral concern for Lutherans; so much, in fact, that many seem not to have healthy attitudes regarding sexual relations even after marriage.

Although Lutherans feel strongly about particular moral

issues in American society, they rarely act in an organized way to change the conditions that disturb them. The vast majority of laymen do not see a role for the church in solving problems outside of the institution of religion. This is consistent with the Lutheran ethic, with individuals primarily attempting to live with, or adapt to, the evil conditions of this world while focusing on the next. The Lutheran ethic condemns action in the world as "good works," "legalism," and "lack of humbleness and thus a lack of faith." The ideology makes no specific ethical demands on Lutherans, other than individualistic moral conduct. Weber's charge that Luther did not "establish a new or in any way fundamental connection between worldly activity and religious principles" is supported by this study.[1]

For the theologically conservative and religiously most committed laymen and clergy, views on divorce, the role of women, the treatment of deviance, capital punishment, premarital and extramarital sex, the new morality, and the teaching of birth control are compatible with the theoretical model of the Lutheran ethic and Old Testament Law. Liberal clergymen strongly deviate from the Lutheran ethic on many morality issues, and their moral attitudes differ significantly from the attitudes of the average laymen.

Current Morality

Those individuals most exemplifying the Lutheran ethic —the theologically conservative and religiously committed —would be expected to be the most critical of prevailing morals in America. To test this proposition laymen and clergy were given a choice of five views of the current state of morals, and they most frequently chose "They are bad and getting worse" (Table A-26) . Those choosing this alternative range from 57 percent (LCA) to 69 percent (MS and WS) among laymen, and from 47 percent (LCA) to 86 percent (WS) among clergy. A familiar trend occurs again: the LCA and ALC clergymen are more optimistic than all four of the lay groups, and the MS and WS clergymen are more pessimistic about present-day morality than all the laymen.

Among laymen the judgment that morals are "pretty bad and getting worse" varies significantly with the indexes of religious commitment, with the exception of associational involvement and religious knowledge (Table 5-1). The higher one ranks on the Religious Beliefs, Communal Involvement, and Religious Practices indexes, the more likely he is to hold to a pessimistic view of morals. The largest difference, however, occurs among the clergy in relation to religious beliefs, with the theologically most conservative (those ranking high) most likely to say that morals are "pretty bad and getting worse" (86 percent).

Lutheran women show more pessimism about the present state of morals than men, and 71 percent of the women say morals are getting worse, as opposed to only 54 percent of the men. The traditional double standard between the sexes may partially explain the differences. Social class varies inversely with the belief that morals are "pretty bad and getting worse," with 72 percent of the lower class, 63 percent of the middle class, and 47 percent of the upper class Lutherans choosing this answer.

Dancing

Dancing traditionally has been a debatable moral issue for Lutherans. Some Lutheran bodies have completely opposed social dancing, while in others only particular ministers have disapproved of it. Today few laymen oppose dancing, with 95 percent of the LCA and ALC, 90 percent of the WS, and 89 percent of the MS laymen saying it is not wrong. Fifty-six percent of the MS and only 7 percent of the WS clergy give the same response.

TABLE 5-1
Clergy and Laymen Agreeing that "Morals Are Pretty Bad and Getting Worse," By Type and Degree of Religious Commitment

Sample	Index	Ranking	Agree, By Percentage
Clergy	Beliefs ($p = .001$)	Low	49
		Moderate	59
		High	86
Lay	Beliefs ($p = .001$)	Low	52
		Moderate	64
		High	74
Lay	Associational Involvement ($p = $ NS)	Low	64
		Moderate	67
		High	62
Lay	Communal Involvement ($p = .01$)	Low	59
		Moderate	65
		High	71
Lay	Practices ($p = .01$)	Low	58
		Moderate	61
		High	72
Lay	Knowledge ($p = $ NS)	Low	68
		Moderate	58
		High	68

The Lutheran Ethic

The religious beliefs of both laymen and clergy, and religious practices of laymen, relate to views on dancing (Table A-27). The largest differences occur with the clergy Religious Beliefs Index, where 97 percent ranking low, 77 percent ranking moderate, and 42 percent ranking high on the index view dancing as not wrong.

Aside from the theologically conservative Lutherans, older clergymen often see dancing as morally corrupting. Eighty-eight percent age 30 and under, 81 percent between ages 31 and 40, 58 percent between ages 41 and 50, 56 percent between ages 51 and 60, and 41 percent age 61 and over regard dancing as not wrong. When age is held constant, however, the relationship between theological stance and attitudes toward dancing continues to exist at every age level.

SMOKING

In comparison to dancing, smoking has only recently been conceived of as a moral problem, since researchers have found evidence of its danger to health. About half of the laymen see smoking as "not wrong," with no meaningful differences among the four Lutheran bodies. Approximately 50 percent of the LCA, ALC, and MS clergy and 60 percent of the WS clergy do not see smoking as wrong.

Clergy answering always wrong include 19 percent in the LCA, 7 percent in the ALC, 6 percent in the MS, and none in the WS. Thus the clergymen from the theologically most liberal Lutheran body (LCA) are more likely to see smoking as a moral issue than the clergymen from the theologically most conservative body (WS). On the whole, considerably more laymen than clergymen believe smoking is always wrong, although in no case do the lay percentages exceed one-fourth. None of the dimensions of religious

commitment for either laymen or clergy corresponds meaningfully with their views on smoking, suggesting that for
Lutherans this is not a religious issue. Nearly half the clergy-

TABLE 5-2
Lay and Clergy Attitudes on Divorce, By Branch of Lutheranism

	Sample	By Percentage			
		LCA	ALC	MS	WS
Although never a totally satisfactory answer to family problems, divorce is often the best solution. (Disagreeing)	Lay ($p = .05$)	23	37	41	48
	Clergy ($p = .001$)	28	17	45	81
Do you think a Lutheran minister should agree to perform the marriage of a divorced person? (No)	Lay ($p = $ NS)	10	8	14	17
	Clergy ($p = $ NS)	2	0	5	6

men say that they smoke, a factor which may explain their
attitudes.

DIVORCE

Contrary to liberalized attitudes toward divorce in America today, the Lutheran ethic strongly opposes the breaking
of marital bonds. Two issues were raised to investigate
Lutherans' opinions about divorce (Table 5-2). On the
question "Although never a totally satisfactory answer to
family problems, divorce is often the best solution" (agree
or disagree), the results vary. Only small differences appear
among the four Lutheran bodies, although the clergymen
are consistently more liberal than the laymen. Interestingly,
while 81 percent of the WS clergy disagree that divorce is
often the best solution to family problems, only 17 percent

of the ALC clergy answer this way. Clergymen are consistently more liberal than laymen about performing the marriage of a divorced person, and few differences appear among the four bodies.

When compared by type and degree of religious commitment, Lutherans' opinions on divorce differ significantly only in connection with religious beliefs and communal involvement (Table A-28). Thus, a more conservative stand on divorce relates to a theologically conservative belief system and to greater integration into the Lutheran subcommunity.

SECULAR ROLE OF WOMEN

The changing role of women, one of the most important and controversial social changes in Western civilization over the last century, conflicts with the traditional patriarchal elements of the Lutheran ethic. In the partriarchally-centered family, the husband exclusively plays the role of provider and dominates the decision-making. To determine the extent to which Lutherans still follow the traditional orientations two statements were presented (Table 5-3).

On the question of combining marriage and a career no significant differences appear among the four lay groups, but among the clergymen the percentages agreeing range from 17 in the LCA to 75 in the WS. On the question of family decision-making statistically meaningful differences exist in both the lay and clergy samples. For example, a low of 9 percent of the LCA and a high of 63 percent of the WS clergy do not believe that the wife should have as much to say as the husband in decision-making.

The more conservative an individual's belief system and the greater his degree of communal involvement, the more likely he perceives conflicts between the roles of wife-mother and career woman (Table A-29). Differences by type of religious commitment show up in an even more dramatic

TABLE 5-3
Lay and Clergy Attitudes on the Secular Role of Women,
By Branch of Lutheranism

| | | By Percentage | | | |
	Sample	LCA	ALC	MS	WS
Women who really desire full time careers should not marry because the roles of wife-mother and career woman are basically incompatible. (Agreeing)	Lay (p = NS)	39	42	48	43
	Clergy (p = .001)	17	30	29	75
In the modern family, the wife should have as much to say as the husband in making family decisions. (Disagreeing)	Lay (p = .01)	5	9	9	19
	Clergy (p = .001)	9	13	38	63

way on the question relating to equalitarian decision-making. On religious beliefs, practices, knowledge, and communal involvement, generally the higher an individual ranks, the more often he disagrees with the wife's having as much to say as the husband. Associational involvement is not a significant factor.

Lutheran men see conflicts between the roles of wife-mother and career woman more than do women. Fifty percent of the men, as compared to 39 percent of the women, say the two roles conflict. Regarding equalitarian decision-making, Lutheran men and women show fewer differences (8 and 12 percent disagreeing, respectively). Also, the higher one's social class, the more liberal he is on the secular role of women. When social class is controlled, the previous relationships involving the various aspects of religious commitment still exist.

Treatment of Deviance

Capital Punishment, Sex Criminals, and Homosexuality

Capital punishment is a moral issue that continues to stir major controversy among religious leaders and church members. The Lutheran ethic supports a penalty of death for a person who takes the life of another. When asked whether convicted murderers should be given the death penalty, approximately half the laymen say yes with only small variances among the four lay groups. Clergymen show very wide differences, with 17 percent in the LCA, 43 percent in the ALC, 79 percent in the MS, and 100 percent in the WS agreeing that convicted murderers should be given the death penalty. The clergy, as compared to the laity, hold both the most liberal and the most conservative attitudes, and the findings suggest that the Biblical literalism of the Old Testament "eye for an eye" philosophy (Exodus 21:24) still prevails among the clergymen in the theologically conservative branches.

In addition to advocating the death penalty for murderers, the theologically conservative clergymen more often recommend extreme forms of punishment for other types of deviance. In reaction to the statement "Prison is too good for sex criminals; they ought to be publicly whipped or worse," only minor differences exist in responses among the four lay groups, although more than one-third of the laymen agree with this archaic form of punishment. The four clergy groups show marked differences by Lutheran branch, with the percentages approving such punishment ranging from 2 percent in the LCA, 4 percent in the ALC, 11 percent in the MS, to 25 percent in the WS.

The Lutheran ethic strongly condemns homosexuality. Theologically conservative laymen and clergy agree more

readily than liberals with the statement: "Homosexuals are
to be condemned and should be put in prison." Significant
differences appear among the four Lutheran bodies for both
samples. The percentages of laymen agreeing with the state-

TABLE 5-4
*Lay and Clergy Rankings on Treatment of Deviance Index,
By Branch of Lutheranism*

Sample	Branch	Low	By Percentage Moderate	High
Lay (ρ = NS)	LCA	32	36	32
	ALC	37	32	31
	MS	31	36	33
	WS	28	31	41
Clergy (ρ = .001)	LCA	80	17	3
	ALC	52	40	8
	MS	20	53	27
	WS	5	24	71

ment range from 22 percent in the ALC, 32 percent in the
LCA, 34 percent in the MS, to 38 percent in the WS. The
clergy show much larger differences, with 8 percent of the
LCA, 11 percent of the ALC, 22 percent of the MS, and
75 percent of the WS agreeing. Table A-30 shows responses
to the questions on homosexuality, capital punishment, and
punishment of sex criminals according to type of religious
commitment.

The Treatment of Deviance Index

The questions on the type of treatment that Lutherans
believe convicted murderers, sex criminals, and homosexuals should receive formed the bases for the Treatment

of Deviance Index.[2] A high ranking on the index indicates approval of the most severe punishments (Table 5-4). Few differences exist among the laymen in the four bodies, but

TABLE 5-5

Laymen Ranking High on the Treatment of Deviance Index,
By Rankings on the Religious Knowledge Index, Controlled for Social Class

Class	Religious Knowledge Ranking	Ranking High, By Percentage
Lower	Low	62 (81)
	Moderate	48 (100)
	High	32 (68)
Middle	Low	49 (107)
	Moderate	31 (159)
	High	23 (188)
Upper	Low	27 (11)
	Moderate	19 (59)
	High	13 (52)

in concurrence with previous trends the WS has the largest percentage of laymen ranking high (41 percent) and the smallest percentage ranking low (28 percent) on the index. The differences among the clergy are greater, and those ranking high on the Treatment of Deviance Index are most often in the WS (71 percent) and least often in the LCA (5 percent).

Only two indexes of religious commitment—religious beliefs for clergy and religious knowledge for laymen— show significant links to rankings on the Treatment of Deviance Index (Table A-31). The theologically more liberal a clergyman, the more liberal he tends to be on treatment of deviance. An inverse relationship exists for laymen. The religiously more knowledgeable laymen less often approve harsh treatment of deviants.

Social class influences a respondent's ranking on the Treatment of Deviance Index, with forty-eight percent of the lower class, 32 percent of the middle class, and 17 percent of the upper class laymen ranking high. The relationship between greater religious knowledge and tolerant attitudes on the treatment of deviance remains with social class controlled (Table 5-5). Apparently the religiously more knowledgeable individuals adopt values of compassion and tolerance from the New Testament (such as in Matthew 5:38-39), rather than emphasizing harsh treatment, which the least knowledgeable laymen and the theologically conservative clergymen derive from the Old Testament (such as in Exodus 21:12-24).

SEX AND VIOLENCE IN THE MASS MEDIA

More than 90 percent of the laymen think that publications dwelling on sex and using obscene language should be banned from the newsstand. Likewise, more than 80 percent of the laymen say they are disturbed by the amount of violence and sex in movies and on television, with only minimal differences among the four bodies. The issue disturbs nearly as many clergy as laymen—74 percent of the LCA, 83 percent of the ALC, 85 percent of the MS, and 93 percent of the WS.

An individual's degree of religious commitment corresponds strongly to his answer to this question (Table A-32). Every index reveals significant differences, with the exception of the clergy on religious beliefs and the laymen on religious knowledge. On all the other indexes the higher an individual ranks, the more likely he objects to sex and violence in movies and television. The objection is greater among Lutheran women than men, with ninety-two percent of the women, as compared to 74 percent of the men, indicating concern.

Lutherans who expressed concern about the problem

were asked if they had ever tried to do *anything* about it. Fifty percent in the LCA, 56 percent in the ALC, 74 percent in the MS, to 77 percent in the WS clergymen say yes. However, less than one-fourth of the laymen in all branches have done anything. Thus, while laymen may be quite concerned about a moral issue, few have ever tried to change the situation.

Responses of concern about the problem by types and degrees of religious commitment appear in Table A-33. Significantly, the theologically more conservative the clergymen, and the more highly-ranked the laymen on religious practices and knowledge, the more often they report attempts to do something about the problem. Also, the higher an individual's social class, the more likely he is to have taken some action. Fourteen percent of the lower class, 20 percent of the middle class, and 44 percent of the upper class Lutherans said that they had tried to do something about this issue.

Those who had taken action were asked *what* it was that they had done. The responses were categorized into three types of actions: indirect action, direct individual action, and direct group action (Table A-34) .[3] Only a few notable differences exist among the four Lutheran groups. Among the WS clergy 100 percent of the answers fall under the indirect action category, as compared to 70 percent of the MS, 63 percent of the LCA, and 59 percent of the ALC clergy. The WS includes 60 percent of the clergy who have preached about it, 10 percent who have taught or lectured against it, 10 percent who have prayed about it, 10 percent who have discussed the issue with an individual or a group, and finally 10 percent who have worked on a review committee. Of Lutherans who say they have tried to do something about this problem the large majority mention indirect actions, not active attempts to change the situation, but rather measures to adjust to or live with the problem. Well over half of the laymen report avoidance items ("turn off TV," "don't attend movies," "selective viewing," "pro-

TABLE 5-6
*Lay and Clergy Attitudes on Premarital and Extramarital Sex,
By Branch of Lutheranism*

		By Percentage			
	Sample	LCA	ALC	MS	WS
It is all right for a person to engage in sexual relations before marriage with the person he or she intends to marry. (Agreeing)	Lay ($p = .05$)	17	17	13	8
	Clergy ($p = .05$)	13	17	17	6
Women who engage in premarital sexual relations are almost certain to have serious emotional difficulties in marriage. (Disagreeing)	Lay ($p = $ NS)	36	43	35	37
	Clergy ($p = .05$)	46	49	40	25
It is possible that a particular situation could justify extramarital relations. (Agreeing)	Lay ($p = .05$)	26	22	16	19
	Clergy ($p = .001$)	44	30	17	6

tect children from such things"), and approximately another one-fifth simply have discussed the problem. Most noticeable is the very small percentage of laymen and clergy involved in any organized group effort to actively attack the problem. The impact of the Lutheran ethic is obvious. LCA and ALC clergymen report the most group action.

PREMARITAL AND EXTRAMARITAL SEX

The Lutheran ethic prescribes that premarital and extramarital sexual relations are explicitly and unquestionably wrong. Lutherans generally hold conservative views on the subjects, as revealed by their responses to three questions (Table 5-6). Here the data show that only a small minority of the laymen and clergy feel that premarital sex is permissible, even with the person one intends to marry. On the question of whether premarital sexual relations will lead

TABLE 5-7
*Lay and Clergy Rankings on the New Morality Index,
By Branch of Lutheranism*

Sample	Branch	Low	By Percentage Moderate	High
Lay ($p =$ NS)	LCA	36	42	22
	ALC	37	42	21
	MS	46	36	18
	WS	44	41	15
Clergy ($p = .01$)	LCA	35	31	34
	ALC	37	33	30
	MS	46	34	20
	WS	63	37	0

to serious emotional problems slightly more than one-third of the laymen say no, with only minor differences among the branches. Although the clergy percentages are somewhat larger, in every lay and clergy group the majority see serious emotional problems arising from premarital sex. Only from 16 to 26 percent of the laymen believe that a particular situation could justify extramarital relations. In the four clergy groups 44 percent of the LCA, 30 percent of the ALC, 17 percent of the MS, and 6 percent of the WS clergymen agree.

These attitudes relate to almost every type of religious orientation, with the most marked differences found in connection with the clergy on the Religious Beliefs Index (Table A-35). For example, 63 percent of the theologically liberal clergy, compared with 31 percent of the conservative, do not think that premarital sex will lead to serious emotional difficulties. On the question concerning extra-

TABLE 5-8
Clergy and Lay Rankings on the New Morality Index,
By Type and Degree of Religious Commitment

Sample	Index	Ranking	By Percentage		
			Low	Moderate	High
Clergy	Beliefs ($p = .001$)	Low	18	28	54
		Moderate	48	33	19
		High	57	38	5
Lay	Beliefs ($p = .001$)	Low	30	42	28
		Moderate	37	44	19
		High	54	33	13
Lay	Associational Involvement ($p = .001$)	Low	27	45	28
		Moderate	46	38	16
		High	49	37	14
Lay	Communal Involvement ($p = .001$)	Low	34	42	24
		Moderate	41	41	18
		High	55	30	15
Lay	Practices ($p = .001$)	Low	33	40	27
		Moderate	39	42	19
		High	50	38	12
Lay	Knowledge ($p = .01$)	Low	36	38	26
		Moderate	39	41	20
		High	46	41	13

marital sex more than a majority of the liberal clergy think that extramarital sexual relations can be justified, in contrast to only 5 percent of the theologically most conservative.

The New Morality Index

The three questions on sexual behavior are a measure of the attitudes of Lutherans toward the sexual revolution or the so-called new sexual morality in the United States. A New Morality Index, giving one point for each liberal answer, was constructed in the manner of other indexes.[4] Theologically more conservative Lutheran bodies tend to be more conservative on new morality (Table 5-7).

The higher a layman or clergyman ranks on every index of religious commitment, the less likely he is to rank high (liberal) on the New Morality Index and the more likely he is to favor traditional sexual norms (Table 5-8). The largest differences are among the clergy in terms of religious beliefs, where 54 percent ranking low (theologically liberal), 19 percent moderate, and 5 percent high also rank high on the New Morality Index.

Likely as a result of the sexual double standard in American society, a larger proportion of men than women rank high on the New Morality Index (31 percent and 12 percent). Age also relates to one's ranking, with younger Lutherans ranking more liberal. Laymen ranking low (conservative) on new morality include 32 percent age 30 and under, 36 percent age 31 to 40, 41 percent age 41 to 50, 45 percent age 51 to 60, and 53 percent over 61. For clergymen, 38 percent age 30 and under, rank conservative, 39 percent age 31 to 40, 40 percent age 41 to 50, 47 percent age 51 to 60, and the most dramatic increase—64 percent over age 61. Controls for age do not erase the relationships between religious commitment and rankings on the index.

The lower the social class of a layman, the more often he

expresses conservative attitudes on sexual behavior. Forty-seven percent of the lower class, 42 percent of the middle class, and 26 percent of the upper class rank low on the New Morality Index. The fact that relationships remain when social class is controlled illustrates the independence of the religious commitment variables. Table A-37 demonstrates the strength of the religious commitment variables by comparing the rankings on the Religious Practices Index with the low rankings on the New Morality Index, with social class controlled. Although the sample contains few non-whites, Negro Lutherans and white Lutherans have strikingly different attitudes about the new morality. Forty-one percent of the Negroes and 19 percent of the whites rank high (most liberal) on the index.

Sex in Marriage

The majority of Lutherans show strong concern about sex in publications, movies, and on television, and they also express traditional opinions about premarital and extramarital sexual relations. The conservative opinions may conceivably carry over into an individual's attitudes relating to sex during marriage. To test for this respondents were asked to agree or disagree with the statement: "Because of the religious nature of marriage, sexual relations between husband and wife should be carried out with restraint."

From 32 percent of the ALC to 42 percent of the MS laymen agree (Table 5-9). Thus, more than one-third of the laymen feel that restraint in sexual intercourse is appropriate even after marriage. The percentages of clergymen agreeing with the statement equal approximately one-half of the lay percentages. Interestingly, while 38 percent of all laymen and 20 percent of all clergy agree, only 8 percent of the Lutherans in the college student sample do. The data reveal a morality gap between the generations, as well as between adult laymen and clergy.

A high or moderate ranking on the Religious Beliefs

TABLE 5-9
Lay and Clergy Attitudes on Sex in Marriage, Sex Standards, and Birth Control, By Branch of Lutheranism

	Sample	By Percentage			
		LCA	ALC	MS	WS
Because of the religious nature of marriage, sexual relations between husband and wife should be carried out with restraint. (Agreeing)	Lay (p = NS)	37	32	42	41
	Clergy (p = NS)	17	24	20	19
In the area of sex relations, traditional religious standards are no longer adequate. (Disagreeing)	Lay (p = .01)	53	50	49	66
	Clergy (p = .001)	27	57	70	94
Good sex education in high school should include knowledge of methods of birth control. (Disagreeing)	Lay (p = .01)	28	30	34	43
	Clergy (p = .001)	15	15	35	88

Index (conservative) corresponds with the view among laymen and clergy that sexual relations in marriage should be carried out with restraint (Table A-38). A similar pattern appears for communal involvement—the highly involved more often agreeing. The only other meaningful differences appear for the Religious Knowledge Index. Here an *inverse* relationship occurs, with those ranking higher in religious knowledge being *less* likely to think that sexual activity between marriage partners should in some way be limited for religious reasons.

Older Lutherans are much more likely to say that sexual relations between husband and wife should be carried out with restraint (Table 5-10). Thus, while 63 percent of the laymen and 64 percent of the clergy age 61 and over agree with the statement, only 26 percent of the laymen and 9 percent of the clergy age 30 and under do. Social classes is an important variable, and 53 percent of the lower class, 34 percent of the middle class, and 25 percent of the upper class respondents agree that restraint should be exercised.

TABLE 5-10
Lay and Clergy Attitudes on Sex in Marriage, By Age
"Because of the Religious Nature of Marriage, Sexual Relations between Husband and Wife Should be Carried Out with Restraint: *Agree*

| Age | By Percentage | |
	Lay	Clergy
30 and under	26	9
31 – 40	27	8
41 – 50	34	16
51 – 60	50	38
61 and over	63	64
	$p = .001$	$p = .001$

SEX AND TRADITIONAL RELIGIOUS STANDARDS

The previous data suggest that the attitudes of many Lutherans toward sex may be so rigid as to hinder normal sexual relationships in married life. Although this study did not attempt to make such a measurement, many Lutherans may harbor considerable guilt about sexual matters. All societies, of course, must have rules governing sexual behavior. But if the rules are too harsh or produce extensive guilt, then perhaps a reevaluation is necessary.

The study did evaluate Lutherans' attitudes toward change in traditional religious standards governing sex relations. When asked to react to the statement "In the area of sex relations, traditional religious standards are no longer adequate," laymen decisively disagree (Table 5-9). The clergymen exhibit vast differences of opinion, with from 27 percent in the LCA to 94 percent in the WS disagreeing.

An individual's religious belief system is again important, with differences more striking among the clergy than laymen (Table A-38). Twenty-five percent of the clergymen ranking low, 60 percent moderate, and 84 percent high on the Religious Beliefs Index believe that traditional religious sex standards are adequate. A liberal theological position apparently engenders acceptance of a more liberal sexual code.

Theologically conservative clergymen tend to oppose any changes in traditional religious standards governing behavior, not just those relating to sex. For example, in reacting to the statement "The unchanging Law of God is an absolute standard by which to measure man's conduct," 45 percent of the LCA, 69 percent of the ALC, 87 percent of the MS, and 100 percent of the WS clergymen agree. Also, 39 percent ranking low, 77 percent moderate, and 97 percent high on the Religious Beliefs Index agree with this expression of the unchanging Law of God.

BIRTH CONTROL INFORMATION

A final question dealing with attitudes on sexual morality relates to sex education. Lutherans were asked to agree or disagree with the statement "Good sex education in high school should include knowledge on methods of birth control." Among both laymen and clergy the more conservative branches of Lutheranism have a higher percentage of individuals disagreeing (Table 5-9). Among the clergy, only 15 percent in the LCA and ALC disagree, as compared to 88 percent in the WS.

The Religious Beliefs, Practices, Associational Involve-

ment, and Communal Involvement indexes all show trends
suggesting that the higher an individual ranks, the more he
opposes instruction in high schools on birth control methods (Table A-38). Theological stance for both clergy and
laity is the most significant factor in attitudes on the dis-
semination of birth control information in high schools.
The evidence supports the contention that theologically
conservative individuals encourage opposition to sex education programs in public schools.

ABORTION

Abortion is currently a hotly debated issue throughout
the United States. Many state legislatures are considering
bills which will greatly liberalize existing abortion laws,
and a few have already passed such measures. To ascertain
the attitudes of Lutherans on abortion, the survey asked laymen and clergy to react to the statement "A woman should
have the right to get an abortion if she does not want to
bring a child into the world."

Significant differences on this question occur among the
four Lutheran bodies for both samples. Among the laymen,
67 percent in the LCA, 71 percent in the ALC, 75 percent
in the MS, and 80 percent in the WS disagree that a woman
should be able to have an abortion if she wants one. Larger
differences appear among the clergymen, where 57 percent
in the LCA, 82 percent in the ALC, 92 percent in the MS,
and 100 percent in the WS disagree. On this issue the LCA
clergy are more liberal and the ALC, MS, and WS clergy
more conservative than the laymen from all four Lutheran
bodies.

In almost every case the higher an individual ranks on
any index of religious commitment, the more likely he believes that a woman should not be able to get an abortion

(Table 5-11). Interestingly, women (77 percent) more often than men (67 percent) oppose abortion. Also, the

TABLE 5-11
Lay and Clergy Attitudes on Abortion, By Type and Degree of Religious Commitment

Sample	Index	Ranking	"A Woman Should Have the Right to Get an Abortion if She Does not Want to Bring a Child into the World": (Disagreeing, By Percentage)
Clergy	Beliefs ($p = .001$)	Low	62
		Moderate	85
		High	96
Lay	Beliefs ($p = .001$)	Low	57
		Moderate	74
		High	85
Lay	Associational Involvement ($p = .01$)	Low	65
		Moderate	83
		High	80
Lay	Communal Involvement ($p = .01$)	Low	68
		Moderate	73
		High	83
Lay	Practices ($p = .01$)	Low	67
		Moderate	72
		High	79
Lay	Knowledge ($p = .05$	Low	68
		Moderate	71
		High	78

higher an individual's social class, the more likely he approves of the right to have an abortion. Eighty percent of the Lutherans classified as lower class, 75 percent middle class, and 62 percent upper class oppose abortion. The issue clearly illustrates the discriminating effects of social class and religious commitment. Whereas a higher social class standing corresponds with liberal attitudes on abortion, great religious commitment and theological conservatism correspond with conservative attitudes.

Sale of Guns

In the United States a large portion of the population owns guns. The widespread possession of firearms has an obvious influence on murder and robbery rates, as well as accidental injuries and deaths. Lutherans were questioned about their opinions on Congressional restrictions of gun sales and the role that the church should play in gun control.

Laymen opposing gun legislation range from only 19 to 24 percent, but the clergymen vary considerably by branch of Lutheranism (Table 5-12). Whereas only 13 percent of the LCA clergy oppose gun control legislation, 60 percent of the WS clergy do. More than two-thirds of the laymen see no role for the church in connection with gun control. The clergymen, however, diverge widely, with 28 percent of the LCA and 93 percent of the WS indicating no role for the church. The attitudes of the LCA clergymen differ most from the majority of the laymen. Females (83 percent), as compared to males (63 percent), more frequently respond that Congress should pass a law restricting gun sales. Women (28 percent) are also much more likely than men (20 percent) to indicate a role for the church concerning the issue.

Laymen's views do not vary meaningfully with their rankings on any of the indexes of religious commitment. However, the more conservative a clergyman's theological stance,

TABLE 5-12

Clergy and Lay Attitudes on the Restriction of Gun Sales and the Church's Role in This Matter, By Branch of Lutheranism

| | | By Percentage | | | |
	Sample	LCA	ALC	MS	WS
Do you think Congress should pass a law restricting and limiting the sale of guns? (No)	Lay ($p =$ NS)	21	24	19	23
	Clergy ($p = .05$)	13	30	30	60
Do you think the church should do anything about this problem? (No)	Lay ($p =$ NS)	67	66	70	75
	Clergy ($p = .001$)	28	42	60	93

the more he opposes Congress' restricting or limiting the sale of guns. Twenty percent ranking low, 25 percent moderate, and 37 percent high on the Religious Beliefs Index oppose gun legislation. In relation to church involvement, even wider differences appear among the clergy. While laymen at all levels on the Religious Beliefs Index strongly oppose church involvement, three out of four of the theologically more liberal clergymen see a role for the church. Twenty-five percent of the clergy ranking low, 47 percent moderate, and 72 percent high on the belief index say the church should not do anything about gun control. The theologically conservative clergymen match the majority of the laymen with their attitudes favoring noninvolvement of the church. Religiously conservative clergymen conceivably may oppose gun legislation for two reasons. First, in accordance with the Lutheran ethic, they may generally oppose legalistic actions attempting to control behavior. Second, many conservative clergymen may stress the American tradition of individualism and the right to defend themselves. A few respondents consider such legislation to be a Communist trick to disarm America.

Auto Accidents

On the issue of automobile accidents and deaths Lutherans answered the question "Last year there were about 50,000 individuals killed on our nation's highways. Do you see any role for the church in lowering this rate?" Considerably fewer laymen than clergy say yes, and only slightly more than one-third of the laity perceive a role for the church, with only small differences among the four groups. In contrast, 95 percent of the MS, 93 percent of the LCA, 89 percent of the ALC, and 75 percent of the WS clergymen answer yes. Table A-43 shows answers by type and degree of religious commitment.

Lutherans who say they see a role for the church in reducing automobile accidents were asked what sort of role they mean. Their responses are grouped into two broad categories (Table A 39); the first includes actions to be taken within the local congregation or within the institution of religion itself, and the second encompasses group action to be taken outside of the institutional church.[5] Almost all actions mentioned by laymen and clergy fall into the category of actions carried out within the institution of religion. Clergymen from the LCA and ALC more often than MS and WS clergymen mention taking actions outside the institutional church. Twenty percent of the LCA, 12 percent of the ALC, 6 percent of the MS, and none of the WS clergymen mention these types of action. The WS members most frequently emphasize items of the first category like stress Fifth Commandment or stress obedience to laws. Otherwise, very few differences appear among the Lutheran groups. Most individuals confine their moral concerns and obligations to the institution of religion, and this compartmentalization of religion results in few Lutherans attempting to change the existing secular social order to attack the problem of auto accidents.

VI

The Institution of Religion

ACCORDING to the Lutheran ethic the function of the church is to preach the gospel, and the primary role of the clergy is proclaiming this message. The church and minister should focus on saving souls for the next world rather than attempting social reform in this world or building the kingdom of God on earth.

Consistent with this, Luther's doctrine of the two kingdoms functions to keep the institution of religion separate from the secular world. The ethic regards all institutions as appointed and controlled by divine providence and directs individuals not to actively seek to change them. To Luther, even if brutal tyrants rule, the Christian must suffer humbly and endure patiently. He favored obedience to all authorities, whether the patriarchal head of the family or the government leaders. The Lutheran ethic principle of nonresistance is reflected in the strong opposition among laymen to civil disobedience. The individual Lutheran seeks personal salvation, but since man's nature is sinful, his only real hope is trusting in God. Good works do not obtain spiritual grace, and individuals receive grace only through the Word the church preaches, and through the sacraments of Holy Communion and Baptism.

This study finds that the theologically conservative and

religiously committed Lutherans favor the traditional views of the roles of the laity, women, the clergy, and the congregation. Most laymen consider the seeking of personal salvation and matters such as church attendance, prayer, Bible reading, and taking Communion as their primary religious obligations. The theologically more conservative and religiously more committed Lutherans are more likely to uphold the practice of patriarchal dominance in the church and thus stress the subordinate role for women that the Lutheran ethic prescribes.

The vast majority of laymen see the role of the clergy as consistent with the doctrine of the separation of the two kingdoms. They do not want their clergymen involved in secular affairs, and a large percentage indicate they will withhold contributions if their clergymen deviate from their prescribed roles. The majority of the LCA and ALC clergy, and many of the MS clergy, however, differ markedly with the laymen on the proper role of the clergy. The theologically liberal clergymen most often oppose the church's confining itself to saving souls for the next world. These gaps in role expectations and institutional goals are a potential source of conflict within the church.

Ideological conservatism among Lutheran laymen and theologically conservative clergymen leads them to resist all types of change, even within the institution of religion. Although many are not happy with particular aspects of the institution, such as its formality and extensive liturgy in worship services, they oppose change. The majority of laymen regard the total church organization and forms as commanded by God and thus as something that must be endured. Apparently the theologically more conservative and committed see Lutheranism as the one true religion and, therefore, believe change within it is undesirable.

ROLE OF THE LAITY

How does the individual Lutheran view his role as a member of a local congregation and in the world outside the church? Several items in this study attempt to answer the question. On the statement "The membership of the church is primarily and basically a group of people to be served or ministered unto by the pastor" considerably more laymen than clergy agree. The lay percentages range from 77 percent in the ALC, 80 percent in the LCA, 83 percent in the MS, to 90 percent in the WS. Thus the data show little evidence of the Lutheran concept of the priesthood of all believers. The clergy percentages are considerably smaller, although a similar trend appears, with 24 percent in the ALC, 32 percent in the LCA, 37 percent in the MS, to 50 percent in the WS agreeing with the statement.

Except for the clergy, type and degree of religious commitment has only a minor influence on an individual's answer. On the clergy Religious Beliefs Index those ranking high (most conservative) agree with almost twice the frequency (44 percent) as those ranking low (23 percent). The most knowledgeable laymen also tend to agree less frequently (79 percent), as compared to the least knowledgeable (89 percent).

Larger portions of older laymen and clergy than younger believe that the membership of the church is primarily a group of people to be served or ministered unto by the pastor (Table 6-1). The views of the older clergymen coincide with the beliefs of the laymen, whereas younger clergymen have a totally different outlook. Lower and middle class Lutherans are more likely to accept the laymen's traditional role than upper class Lutherans. Eighty-six percent of the lower, 85 percent of the middle, and 54 percent of the upper class laymen view the membership of the church as being served or ministered unto by the pastor.

While most laymen depend strongly on their clergymen

TABLE 6-1

Lay and Clergy Attitudes on the Role of the Laity, By Age

"The membership of the church is primarily and basically a group of people to be served or ministered unto by the pastor." (Agreeing)

	By Percentage	
Age	*Lay*	*Clergy*
30 and under	75	12
31-40	81	20
41-50	80	40
51-60	89	41
61 and over	89	83
	$p = .001$	$p = .001$

for their religious needs, the theologically more conservative see their role as laymen primarily as accepting all church creeds, attending church each Sunday, praying and reading the Bible daily, and taking Communion regularly. In contrast, the theologically liberal greatly deemphasize these traditional religious activities. The laymen rated the belief and practice items in Table 6-2 as 1) very important; 2) probably important; 3) probably not important; or 4) not important. The table shows the percentages answering very important to each question.

Laymen show significant differences by Lutheran branch on every question except participating in church activities and organizations and tithing. On all other items, except working for social justice, the theologically more conserva-

TABLE 6-2

What Laymen and Clergy Feel Is "Very Important" for a Lutheran to Believe or Do, By Branch of Lutheranism

By Percentage

Percentage saying it is "very important" to:	Lay				Clergy			
	LCA	ALC	MS	WS	LCA	ALC	MS	WS
Accept all church creeds and doctrines	52 (*p* = .001)	51	61	70	15 (*p* = .001)	24	57	94
Attend church every Sunday	54 (*p* = .001)	58	64	79	50 (*p* = .01)	57	74	100
Be active in church activities and organizations	44 (*p* = NS)	37	43	54	30 (*p* = NS)	6	33	19
Pray daily	76 (*p* = .001)	80	93	92	72 (*p* = .05)	78	92	100
Work for social justice	65 (*p* = .001)	51	47	47	67 (*p* = .001)	70	59	13
Read the Bible daily	50 (*p* = .001)	54	67	67	48 (*p* = .01)	54	79	88
Tithe (give 10 percent of income)	42 (*p* = NS)	33	39	61	32 (*p* = .05)	17	37	13
Be a member of your particular branch of Lutheranism	34 (*p* = .001)	34	52	61	13 (*p* = .001)	6	26	63
Participate regularly in Communion	78 (*p* = .01)	85	91	92	83 (*p* = NS)	89	95	100

tive branches of Lutheranism (particularly the WS) have the largest percentage of members answering very important. Interestingly, however, on the question concerning social justice, the WS has the lowest percentage of the four lay groups answering very important.

The clergy data show significant differences among the four Lutheran bodies on every question except participating in church activities and organizations and participating regularly in Communion, although in the last question a definite trend is apparent. The question on tithing shows no particular trend or pattern. On all the other questions, except the social justice item, the theologically more conservative branches have larger percentages of their clergymen saying very important. The social justice item, however, results in an inverse relationship, with the WS clergy least likely to say that working for social justice is very important (13 percent).

Table A-40 shows answers to the nine questions when the respondents' rankings on the various dimensions of religious commitment are taken into account. Table 6-2, which compares the various branches of Lutheranism, reveals a similar pattern. On every index except religious knowledge the higher an individual ranks, the more likely he is to say that a particular item is very important, except for working for social justice. On this question four of the six indexes of religious commitment show no meaningful differences. On the Religious Practices Index, however, laymen who rank high tend to say that working for social justice is very important. On the other hand, the clergy data for the Religious Beliefs Index indicate an inverse relationship, and the higher one ranks on the index, the less often he believes that working for social justice is very important. This finding corresponds with the data on prejudiced attitudes discussed in Chapter Four.

ROLE OF WOMEN IN THE CHURCH

Probably the most dramatic differences among the clergy found in the entire study relate to impressions about the role of women in the church. On the questions of whether women should have as equal a voice as men in church decisions 98 percent of both the LCA and ALC, 47 percent of the MS, and none of the WS clergy answer affirmatively. Lutheranism traditionally has been patriarchal. According to the Lutheran ethic, while women have spiritual equality in the eyes of God, males should dominate the church.

Lutherans also gave their opinions on whether women should be allowed to become ordained ministers (Table 6-3). Pronounced differences appear among the four bodies for laymen and clergy on the question, although the percentages agreeing are lower than for the church decision-making item. Apparently the equalitarian values prevalent in American society seriously challenge the patriarchal aspect of the Lutheran ethic, except among the theologically most conservative clergymen.

Laymen in the conservative branches of Lutheranism (MS and WS) more willingly grant women greater rights and freedom in the church than do their clergymen. In fact, nearly half of the WS laymen think women should have an equal voice in decision-making, and almost two out of every five approve of women ministers. Lutheran men are significantly more liberal about the role of women in the church than are the women themselves. Seventy-nine percent of the males, as compared to 71 percent of the females, think that women should have an equal voice in church decisions; 65 percent of the men, as compared to 51 percent of the women, think that women should be allowed to become ministers. The answers also vary significantly according to whether one is of German or Scandinavian descent. On both questions those of German background less frequently approve of equality for women. For example, 49 percent of the German, as compared to 68 percent

TABLE 6-3

Lay and Clergy Attitudes on the Role of Women in the Church, By Branch of Lutheranism

		By Percentage			
	Sample	LCA	ALC	MS	WS
Do you think women should have as equal a voice in church decisions as men? (Yes)	Lay ($p = .001$)	91	86	71	49
	Clergy ($p = .001$)	98	98	47	0
Should women be allowed to become ordained ministers? (Yes)	Lay ($p = .001$)	73	68	47	39
	Clergy ($p = .001$)	62	30	8	0

of the Scandinavian Lutherans, believe that women should be allowed to be ordained. Finally, except for one index, the higher an individual ranks on a particular dimension of commitment, the less likely he is to say yes on each question (Table 6-4). Thus, a conservative theological stance, and greater religious commitment and involvement, relate strongly to preference of a restricted role for women in the church.

ROLE OF THE CLERGY

Traditionally the primary responsibility of the Lutheran clergyman has been preaching the Gospel. However, in recent years many Protestant clergymen have questioned such a simplified designation of the clergyman's role and have gone into the secular world, challenging major social institutions and individuals in power. The actions have caused considerable conflict among both clergy and laymen.[1] Three important findings emerge concerning the role of the clergy. First, most laymen and the theologically

TABLE 6-4

Clergy and Lay Attitudes on the Role of Women in the Church,
By Type and Degree of Religious Commitment

Sample	Index	Ranking	By Percentage	
			Women should have as equal a voice in church decisions (Yes)	Women be allowed to become ordained ministers (Yes)
Clergy	Beliefs	Low	96	50
		Moderate	85	28
		High	34	2
			$(p = .001)$	$(p = .001)$
Lay	Beliefs	Low	91	70
		Moderate	80	62
		High	54	38
			$(p = .001)$	$(p = .001)$
Lay	Associational Involvement	Low	80	64
		Moderate	76	59
		High	67	47
			$(p = .01)$	$(p = .001)$
Lay	Communal Involvement	Low	83	62
		Moderate	74	58
		High	60	43
			$(p = .001)$	$(p = .001)$
Lay	Practices	Low	83	64
		Moderate	76	60
		High	64	47
			$(p = .001)$	$(p = .001)$
Lay	Knowledge	Low	84	60
		Moderate	78	65
		High	63	46
			$(p = .001)$	$(p = .001)$

liberal clergy differ widely in interpreting a clergyman's role. Second, white and Negro Lutherans have varying views on the proper role of the clergy. Finally, younger

TABLE 6-5
*Lay and Clergy Attitudes on the Role of Clergymen,
By Branch of Lutheranism*

		By Percentage			
	Sample	LCA	ALC	MS	WS
It is all right for ministers and other religious leaders to march and participate in protest demonstrations. (Disagreeing)	Lay ($p = .01$)	65	72	74	83
	Clergy ($p = .001$)	17	19	57	81
Clergy should stick to religion and not concern themselves with social, economic and political problems. (Agreeing)	Lay ($p = .001$)	49	50	45	70
	Clergy ($p = .001$)	6	6	21	67
If clergymen insist on getting involved in political activities or in picketing or demonstrations, church members have every right to withhold or limit their church contributions. (Agreeing)	Lay ($p = $ NS)	33	35	39	34
	Clergy ($p = .05$)	19	9	22	44

Lutherans are more likely than older Lutherans to see the role as extending into social, economic, and political realms. Three questions were included to assess the views of the Lutherans about the role of the clergy (Table 6-5). The first two statements relate directly to roles, and the third considers possible financial sanctions that might be used against clergymen who involve themselves in activities which the members do not approve.

The large majority of the laymen disapprove of ministers' and other religious leaders' participating in protest demonstrations. In contrast, the clergy show a wide variation by branch of Lutheranism, with only 17 percent in the LCA, as compared to 81 percent in the WS, disapproving. The Wisconsin Synod also has the largest percentages of laymen who think that clergymen should stick to religion and not concern themselves with social, economic, and political problems. Again the clergy attitudes strongly differ from those of the laity, except in the WS. On the third question more than one-third of the laymen agree with the idea of withholding or limiting of church contributions if clergymen assume roles which the laymen dislike. A notably higher percentage of the WS clergy (44 percent) approve of the tactic than any other clergy or lay group.

Rankings on the Associational Involvement, Religious Practices, or Religious Knowledge indexes do not relate to views on the role of the clergy (Table A-41). On the other hand, those ranking higher on the Communal Involvement Index, and on the lay and clergy Religious Beliefs indexes, are more conservative about the clergyman's role on social issues. The same trend exists on the withholding of funds for the theologically more conservative clergy and for the laymen ranking higher in communal involvement, but a small inverse relationship exists among the laymen in terms of religious knowledge.

Definitions of the role of the clergy vary widely according to age. Younger laymen and clergy see the minister's role as extending into protest demonstrations and into social, economic, and political issues. Also, the higher a layman's social class, the more likely he is to approve of participation in protest demonstrations and other forms of secular involvement. Lutherans of higher social class less often agree with the idea of withholding contributions.

Negroes accept a tremendously broader view of the role of clergymen. For example, while 75 percent of the white respondents disagree that clergymen should march in protest demonstrations, only 23 percent of the Negroes give this answer. Negroes apparently look to clergymen as social as well as spiritual leaders.[2] Nevertheless, members of inner-city congregations significantly more often suggest withholding or limiting church contributions if clergymen get involved in demonstrations. Forty-six percent of the Lutherans from inner-city churches, 37 percent from outlying sections of the central city, and 33 percent from suburban churches agree with the legitimacy of holding back funds. Inner-city clergymen are the most likely to become involved in protest demonstrations,[3] and thus they are the ones most likely to face threats of financial cutbacks.

ROLE OF THE CONGREGATION

The vast majority of laymen and clergy (only half of the WS clergy, however) believe that their congregations should support special ministries, such as among skid row people, hospitals, the aged, or youth. However, more than two-thirds of the laymen believe that these things should be done only after the needs of the congregation's own members have been served (Table 6-6). Considerably fewer clergy than laymen—especially in the LCA and ALC—think that the primary responsibility of the local congregation is to serve the needs of its own membership. The final question in Table 6-6 deals with the matter of autonomy of the local congregation. The issue provokes vigorous debate among church leaders and is one of the major barriers preventing Lutheran churches from developing more cooperative ministries in metropolitan areas. Although the differences are not statistically significant, more laymen from the theologically more conservative bodies are slightly less favorable toward congregational autonomy than those from the more liberal branches. No meaningful trend exists among the four clergy groups.

Religious commitment in some cases varies significantly with one's views of the congregation's role (Table A-42). On the issue of the congregation's serving the needs of

TABLE 6-6
Lay and Clergy Attitudes on the Role of the Congregation, By Branch of Lutheranism

		By Percentage			
	Sample	LCA	ALC	MS	WS
All Lutheran congregations should contribute to the support of certain forms of ministry in the city such as to skid row people, hospitals, the aged or youth. (Disagreeing)	Lay ($p = .001$)	7	4	12	29
	Clergy ($p = .001$)	7	7	10	50
The primary responsibility of the local congregation is to serve the needs of its membership before serving the needs of those outside the church. (Agreeing)	Lay ($p = .05$)	67	67	76	78
	Clergy ($p = .01$)	27	35	47	50
A local church should have the right to make final decisions regarding its future and ministry without interference from synod or district. (Agreeing)	Lay ($p = $ NS)	58	53	49	46
	Clergy ($p = .05$)	30	43	52	44

members before serving those outside the church, meaningful variances show up for laymen and clergy in terms of religious beliefs and communal involvement. The higher an individual ranks on these indexes, the more readily he puts the needs of the members first. On the issue of supporting certain special forms of ministry, significant differences occur only on the lay and clergy Religious Beliefs and the Communal Involvement indexes. The higher one ranks on the indexes, the more likely he opposes such action. On the local autonomy question an interesting pattern prevails. For the laymen significant differences emerge on all but the Communal Involvement Index, and individuals ranking higher on any other index less frequently favor congregational autonomy. However, among the clergy in terms of religious beliefs the exact opposite pattern emerges, with the more conservative clergymen supporting local congregational autonomy.

In summary, Lutheran laymen more than the clergy see the local congregation as serving its own members before providing for the needs of those outside the church. This is particularly true for those deeply involved in the Lutheran subcommunity. On the other hand, the majority of Lutherans indicate that congregations should contribute to certain special forms of ministry outside the local congregation. The responses to the two questions do not necessarily conflict. The results merely suggest that the needs of the people outside the local church are lower in priority than the needs of the members. At what point the needs of the congregation are satisfied remains unknown.

The theologically more conservative clergy see interference from synod or district as a restriction on their individual freedom. Theologically liberal clergymen more readily welcome the help of the districts and synods. In contrast, the theologically more liberal laymen want to preserve their congregational autonomy. Most laymen ranking liberal in terms of religious beliefs belong to the LCA and ALC, and it is in these branches that synod and district officials have proposed the most challenging social programs for local congregations. Laymen from these groups see the programs as threats to their own value systems, security, and social well-being and consequently want to maintain control by the local congregation.

RELIGION AND SOCIAL ACTION

Some people see religion as potential force for reforming undesirable conditions in society, believing the church has an obligation to effect change. In this study, however, only a minority of laymen support the idea of the church's becoming involved in social action programs (Table 6-7).

TABLE 6-7
*Lay and Clergy Attitudes on Social Action,
By Branch of Lutheranism*

	Sample	LCA	ALC	MS	WS
		By Percentage			
Denominations should issue policy statements on social and economic matters. (Agreeing)	Lay ($p = .05$)	45	43	40	30
	Clergy ($p = .001$)	95	87	62	13
The church can best contribute to the solution of social problems by preaching the gospel and by winning individuals to salvation. (Disagreeing)	Lay ($p = $ NS)	10	10	4	5
	Clergy ($p = .001$)	48	30	22	0
Church leaders as a group should take a public stand on political issues. (Agreeing)	Lay ($p = $ NS)	25	22	22	17
	Clergy ($p = .001$)	69	57	37	0
The most important thing is the salvation of mankind to eternal life rather than carrying on a social reform program here in this world. (Disagreeing)	Lay ($p = .001$)	29	28	10	8
	Clergy ($p = .001$)	75	43	15	6

Most members, consistent with the Lutheran ethic, conceive of the role of the church as preaching the gospel, with the primary emphasis being eternal salvation in the next world. Laymen from the theologically more conservative branches of Lutheranism more strongly oppose the church's involvement in secular issues, while the clergy responses on involvement reflect widely varying attitudes. For example, on the issue of policy statements on social and economic matters 95 percent of the LCA and 87 percent of the ALC clergy say this is an appropriate church action, compared with 62 percent of the MS and only 13 percent of the WS

TABLE 6-8
Lay and Clergy Rankings on the Social Action Index,
By Branch of Lutheranism

Sample	Branch	Low	By Percentage Moderate	High
Lay ($p = .001$)	LCA	30	63	7
	ALC	33	56	11
	MS	44	53	3
	WS	54	43	3
Clergy ($p = .001$)	LCA	2	33	65
	ALC	4	54	42
	MS	23	55	22
	WS	81	19	0

clergy. On two other questions the WS clergy take a unanimous stand in opposing church involvement in political and social reform activities.

The Social Action Index

On the Social Action Index,[4] developed from the questions in Table 6-7, the WS laymen (54 percent) and clergy (81 percent) have the largest proportions ranking low, or most opposed to social action (Table 6-8). The LCA clergy, on the other hand, have by far the largest percentages ranking high (65 percent).

The higher an individual ranks on almost every index of religious commitment, the more likely he is to rank low on the Social Action Index (Table 6-9). The clergy in terms of religious beliefs show the largest differences, and of the clergymen ranking low (liberal) on the Religious

TABLE 6-9

Clergy and Lay Rankings on the Social Action Index,
By Type and Degree of Religious Commitment

| Sample | Index | Ranking | By Percentage | | |
			Low	Moderate	High
Clergy	Beliefs (p = .001)	Low	2	24	74
		Moderate	11	53	36
		High	35	60	5
Lay	Beliefs (p = .001)	Low	28	62	10
		Moderate	38	56	6
		High	54	45	1
Lay	Associational Involvement (p = .05)	Low	34	60	6
		Moderate	42	53	5
		High	46	48	6
Lay	Communal Involvement (p = .05)	Low	35	58	7
		Moderate	40	54	6
		High	52	47	1
Lay	Practices (p = NS)	Low	37	56	7
		Moderate	42	53	5
		High	42	53	5
Lay	Knowledge (p = .05)	Low	33	60	7
		Moderate	39	55	6
		High	47	49	4

Beliefs Index, 2 percent rank low, 24 percent moderate, and 74 percent high on the Social Action Index. Thus, for clergymen a liberal theological belief system relates strongly

TABLE 6-10
Lay and Clergy Rankings on the Social Action Index, By Age

Age	By Percentage	
	Lay	Clergy
30 and under	6	72
31 – 40	7	45
41 – 50	5	19
51 – 60	4	19
61 and over	6	14
	$p =$ NS	$p = .001$

to attitudes favoring church involvement in social action and social reform.

When age is considered, only minor differences exist among the laymen on the Social Action Index; however, the rankings of the clergy vary markedly by age (Table 6-10). The younger the clergyman, the more likely he favors social action. The differences between the majority of the laymen and the theologically liberal and youthful clergymen may be an indication of tremendous future conflict within the church.

CIVIL DISOBEDIENCE

In accordance with the Lutheran ethic, the majority of laymen oppose breaking the law under any circumstances. Again the laymen differ sharply from the younger, theologically liberal clergymen, who find some types of civil disobedience justified. Lutherans were asked to react to the statement "It is the duty of a good Lutheran to be obedient to secular authorities or the state, and not break laws, no matter what the issue may be." Laymen agreeing range from

TABLE 6-11
Lay and Clergy Attitudes on Civil Disobedience, By Age

	Lutherans should obey secular authorities and not break laws (Agreeing, By Percentage)	
Age	Lay	Clergy
30 and under	71	24
31 — 40	75	35
41 — 50	76	52
51 — 60	87	61
61 and over	88	70
	$p = .001$	$p = .001$

74 (LCA) to 83 percent (MS), with only small differences among the four Lutheran branches. The clergy data reveal large differences among the four Lutheran bodies with 26 percent in the LCA, 33 percent in the ALC, 56 percent in the MS, and 75 percent in the WS stating that they oppose civil disobedience, regardless of the issue. Statistically significant differences in attitudes exist in connection with every index of religious commitment except religious practices and knowledge. On all other indexes the higher an individual ranks, the more he opposes civil disobedience (Table A-45).

Although the differences are much greater for the clergy than the laymen, younger Lutherans more often justify civil disobedience (Table 6-11). Nevertheless, regardless of theological stance or age, the large majority of laymen oppose breaking the law under any conditions.

Another item on civil disobedience included in the clergy questionnaire concerns an incident involving approximately fifty Detroit area clergymen. Early in 1967 the clergymen were arrested for trying to move a Negro family into a house scheduled for demolition in an urban renewal area (known as the Hobart Street incident). The clergymen in the sample commented on the appropriateness of such action in which ministers' engage in civil disobedience. Fifty-six percent of the LCA, 32 percent of the ALC, 9 percent of the MS, and none of the WS approve of breaking the law for what they judge to be a moral cause in the incident. These "moral law breakers" indicate a responsibility to a higher moral law above earthly law.

When variances are analyzed by theological stance, the ministers' reactions are even more dramatic. Eighty-four percent of the theologically most conservative clergy disapprove of the civil disobedience action, while only 2 percent approve. Age also is an important factor. Generally the younger clergymen more often approve of the lawbreaking action and the older clergymen disapprove. Of the clergy age 61 and over 83 percent disapprove and 9 percent approve.

SOCIAL PRONOUNCEMENTS

Only a few laymen know that their church bodies—LCA, ALC, and MS—have made pronouncements on social issues at local and national conventions. An even smaller percentage can correctly identify at least one of these issues. Those who know that pronouncements had been made include 21 percent in the LCA, 13 percent ALC, 13 percent MS, and 7 percent in the WS—interesting, as the WS has made no such pronouncements. Those who can accurately identify at least one issue that their church body has, in reality, spoken on include 11 percent in the LCA and 9 percent in the ALC and MS. Eighty-five percent of these mention a civil rights item. Thus, laymen have practically no awareness of other issues on which the church has spoken.

RELIGIOUS INDIVIDUALISM

Lutheran laymen usually define their religious responsibilities in terms of what may be called religious individualism. As noted, laymen and clergy often have varying role expectations for each other, as well as for the local congregation. Though theologically liberal clergymen would like to see their congregations involved in social action, the large majority of the laymen oppose social reform movements emanating from the church. Using the race problem as an example of a social issue, this study attempted to investigate the type of religious obligation that the layman sees for himself and for his congregation. The issue was worded "Churches can react in many ways to the present situation concerning race relations." The laymen could respond 1) the church and its members should deal with the question only in sermons and/or study groups; 2) individuals may work actively for civil rights on their own, outside of church, but the church should not involve itself directly as a group; and 3) both individuals and church organizations should work actively for the civil rights of all races, even if this means peaceful picketing and demonstrations.

From 19 to 26 percent of the laymen in the four Lutheran bodies prefer confining the issue to sermons or study groups (Table 6-12). Approximately twice as many (41 to 55 percent) consider individual action, but oppose the church's getting involved directly as a group. About one-third of the LCA, ALC, and MS and 18 percent of the WS laymen want both individuals and church groups to work actively for civil rights, even including peaceful

TABLE 6-12
*Lay and Clergy Responses to Types of Race Relations Action,
By Branch of Lutheranism*

Preference	Sample	By Percentage			
		LCA	ALC	MS	WS
The church and its members should deal with the question only in sermons and/or study groups.	Lay	20	19	26	24
	Clergy	4	4	10	13
Individuals may work actively for civil rights on their own outside the church, but the church should not involve itself directly as a group.	Lay	48	45	41	55
	Clergy	11	30	48	88
Both individuals and church organizations should work actively for the civil rights of all races, even if this means peaceful picketing and demonstrations.	Lay	31	34	32	18
	Clergy	83	67	36	0
Don't know.	Lay	1	2	1	3
	Clergy	2	0	6	0

Lay — $p = .01$
Clergy — $p = .001$

picketing and demonstrations. In contrast to the laymen only a small percentage of the clergy (4 to 13 percent) believe the problem should be dealt with just in sermons or study groups. Clergymen stressing religious individualism are primarily from the theologically conservative branches of Lutheranism (88 percent in the WS). The opposite pattern emerges in connection with the approval of both individual and church group action, with 83 percent of the LCA, 67 percent of the ALC, 36 percent of the MS, and none of the WS clergy choosing this alternative.

The most important differences by type and degree of religious commitment again occur among the clergy in connection with religious beliefs (Table A-46). The theologically more conservative clergy prefer individual involvement only, whereas the liberal clergy strongly favor both individuals' and church groups' working for civil rights. Laymen's views do not vary in accordance with their theological stance, associational involvement, or religious practices. However, those ranking higher on the Religious Knowledge Index tend to choose church and individual action, while those ranking higher on the Communal Involvement Index choose this alternative less often.

Although the theologically conservative clergymen stress an individual approach to the problems of race, another question reveals opposition among conservatives to individual action. Ministers were asked to agree or disagree with the statement "I am in basic sympathy with northern ministers and students who have gone to the South to work for civil rights." Seventy-nine percent of the theologically liberal clergy agree, as compared to 59 percent of the moderates and 19 percent of the theologically conservative clergy. Thus, when confronted with a specific response, theologically conservative clergymen most often favor no action at all.

Change in the Institution of Religion

A dramatically changing society presents the institution of religion with the dilemma of either remaining traditional and unchanging or attempting to adapt to the new social order through alterations within the institution itself. Lutheran laymen and clergy were asked whether they think it more important to 1) carry out the traditions of the Lutheran church the way they always have been, or 2) change the church's structure, forms, and services to meet the needs of different times. Twenty-seven percent of the ALC, 38 percent of the LCA, 48 percent of the MS, and 72 percent of the WS laymen feel that it is more important to carry out the traditions of the Lutheran church the way they have always been. Among the clergy 2 percent in the ALC, 6 percent in the LCA, 9 percent in the MS, and 40 percent in the WS give this answer.

In the responses to the question by type and degree of religious commitment each index shows the same trend, except for religious knowledge (Table A-48). The higher an individual ranks on an index, the more likely he opposes change in the church. These data reveal built-in conservative pressures preventing the church from changing. Opinions vary significantly by social class, with the upper class more likely to prefer change in the church and the lower class more likely to oppose it. Fifty-five percent of the lower class, 44 percent of the middle class, and 33 percent of the upper class Lutherans think that carrying out the traditions of the church the way they always have been is most important.

CHANGE IN DOCTRINES AND CREEDS

Although the data have shown that most clergymen approve of change in a general sense, they react much more conservatively to proposals for specific changes in doctrines and creeds. Respondents were asked to agree or disagree with the statements 1) "Church creeds can be expected to change over time," and 2) "Many of the doctrines of the church have little relevance to the modern world." The first statement asks whether individuals regard changing creeds in the institution of religion as natural under changing cultural conditions. The second probes the desire for change from the individual's point of view.

The percentages of laymen disagreeing with the statement on church creeds include 28 percent in the LCA, 40 percent in the ALC, 42 percent in the MS, and 52 percent in the WS. Although the differences between each of the four lay groups reach statistical significance, they are not as great as among the clergy, where 23 percent of the LCA, 39 percent of the ALC, 62 percent of the MS, and 73 percent of the WS clergymen disagree that change is natural. From two-thirds to three-fourths of the laymen disagree that the doctrines of the church have little relevance to the modern world, although no significant differences exist among the four Lutheran bodies. Percentages disagreeing are 67 in the LCA and ALC, 71 in the MS, and 75 in the WS. Among the clergy groups, however, meaningful differences appear, with 42 percent of the LCA, 67 percent of the ALC, 87 percent of the MS, and 100 percent of the WS clergy disagreeing. On every index of religious commitment except one the higher an individual ranks, the more likely he opposes change in creeds and doctrines of the church (Table A-49). The data show that the theologically more conservative and religiously more committed Lutherans are the most ardent supporters of the status quo within the church.

Attitudes Toward Worship Services

Although Lutheran laymen are not completely happy with their worship services, they nevertheless usually oppose changing them. For the majority this conviction comes from the belief that God demands the particular form of service, and thus it is the best possible. These findings are derived from the four questions in Table 6-13. The majority of laymen oppose changing religious forms to attract new members. The percentages of clergymen disagreeing are much lower than for the laity, but once again the Wisconsin Synod (50 percent) has the highest percentage of the four groups disagreeing with the statement. Approximately 50 percent of all the laymen dislike a service with extensive

TABLE 6-13
*Lay and Clergy Attitudes Toward Worship Services,
By Branch of Lutheranism*

		By Percentage			
	Sample	LCA	ALC	MS	WS
Lutheran forms of liturgy, worship services, and hymns should be changed in order to attract new members from different social classes. (Disagreeing)	Lay ($p = .001$)	75	76	82	93
	Clergy ($p = .05$)	30	26	27	50
I tend to like a church service with extensive liturgy and formality. (Disagreeing)*	Lay ($p = $ NS)	55	57	46	48
I like hymns as they are now. (Agreeing)	Lay ($p = $ NS)	69	70	78	77
	Clergy ($p = .05$)	23	15	25	25
The way my Lutheran Church is organized and its services conducted is the way commanded by God and therefore the best possible. (Agreeing)*	Lay ($p = .001$)	52	55	69	73

*Not included on clergy questionnaire.

liturgy and formality, with no meaningful variances among the four Lutheran bodies. The finding is startling, since the typical Lutheran service is very formal and includes extensive liturgy.

The ministers answered a slightly different question and were asked to agree or disagree with the statement "In my opinion ritual and liturgy in the Lutheran church have become almost meaningless and habitual." Nearly half the LCA and ALC clergymen agree with this strong statement, with percentages ranging from 48 percent in the ALC, 45 percent in the LCA, 34 percent in the MS, and 25 percent in the WS. Thus, while half of the laymen do not like church services with extensive liturgy, an average of nearly 40 percent of all the clergy view ritual and liturgy as meaningless and habitual.

Approximately three-quarters of the laymen say they like the Lutheran hymns as they are now and do not want changes in hymns sung. In contrast, from only 15 to 25 percent of the clergymen in the four groups give the same response. This means that while the great majority of the clergy would like to see at least some changes in the hymns sung, an almost identical percentage of laymen seem to want no changes.

The Lutheran ethic's emphasis on acceptance of the status quo apparently also extends to the forms of the church, including services. This may explain the widespread resistance to changes on the part of the laity. It may also explain why laymen continue to attend church services with extensive liturgy and formality despite the fact that half of them dislike such services. On the statement "The way my Lutheran church is organized and its services conducted, is the way commanded by God and, therefore, the best possible" half to three-quarters of the laymen agree.

The theologically more conservative and religiously more committed Lutherans are most likely to defend the existing forms and services, to the extent that members almost deify the forms and think of them as commanded by God. Older laymen most oppose such changes in church forms and see their church services and organization as commanded by God and therefore the best possible. Except for religious practices, those ranking higher on any index of religious commitment more often oppose changes in liturgy, worship services, and hymns (Table A-47). Also, with the exception of religious knowledge, if one ranks high on an index, he prefers formality. On the lay and clergy Religious Beliefs indexes, the Associational Involvement Index, and to some extent on the Communal Involvement Index, the higher an individual ranks, the more likely he is to like the Lutheran hymns as they are now. Finally, on every index of religious commitment, except religious knowledge, those who rank higher are more likely to agree Lutheran forms and services are commanded by God.

A small substudy which was carried out on *The Lutheran Hymnal* supported the previous findings.[5] The year of composition of the words and music of each hymn was recorded, showing that the average years of composition of the words and the music were 1672 and 1682, respectively. Hymns currently sung in Missouri and Wisconsin Synod churches are on the average nearly 300 years old. Approximately 75 percent of the laymen want no changes in the hymns presently sung, a strong indication of how religion is functioning in their lives and of the comfort the hymns seem to give parishioners. The difficult and traditional language in many hymns however, may contribute to the low level of religious knowledge and low theological understanding among the laymen.

VII

Images of Man, God, and Religion

ACCORDING TO the Lutheran ethic, man is innately sinful and evil, and he can never completely overcome his corrupt nature in earthly life. Man's free will is severely restricted, with God the causal force behind all events in this world, as well as in the next. Thus, man is also totally helpless in regard to salvation. Traditional Lutheran theology teaches that salvation comes solely by God's grace, without any merit on the part of individuals.

The Lutheran ethic functions to relieve human suffering and frustration by minimizing rational activity in this world and focusing on the goal of eternal life after death. Luther by no means favored the rise of capitalism or scientific endeavor. He did not consider worldly activity, worldly success, secular education, and intellectual pursuits important in an individual's life plan. Obedient surrender to the God-willed social order and to one's divinely-willed calling was all that was asked.

The vast majority of Lutheran clergymen continue to see man as a naturally sinful creature. While Lutheran laymen take a considerably more optimistic view of man's nature than the clergy, the theologically more conservative and religiously more committed individuals also accept the view of man's nature outlined in the Lutheran ethic. This conception of man's original sinfulness leads to pessimistic views of man's potentials in life and likely has a great bearing on the inactivity of most Lutherans in the secular world.

The theologically more conservative and religiously more committed individuals more often accept the Lutheran view of man as saved by God's grace. However, nearly one-third of the theologically liberal laymen say that man is saved by action and works. Also, in contradiction to the belief that man is saved solely by God's grace, the majority of Lutheran laymen think that people are saved by keeping the Ten Commandments. The clergy almost unanimously disagree.

Theologically conservative clergymen endorse the Lutheran ethic's emphasis on obedience in childrearing. Liberal Lutherans and those less committed to religion more frequently emphasize independent thinking for children. Theologically conservative and religiously more committed individuals see serious conflicts between science and religion, a view reflective of the suspicion of reason and rationality in the Lutheran ethic.

In regard to the function of religion in the lives of Lutherans, salvation is the primary concern of the theologically more conservative and religiously more dedicated Lutherans. Also, the majority seek comfort and security from their religion. The theologically liberal and the religiously less committed more frequently stress moral behavior in their religion.

IMAGES OF MAN

Whether man at birth is regarded as naturally good, evil, or neither of these is a crucial element in any ideology. In Lutheranism, the doctrine of original sin has provided the basic theological image of man. To investigate whether Lutherans still accept this concept of man's original nature the following agree-disagree statements were presented to respondents: 1) "A person at birth is neither good nor bad;"

TABLE 7-1

Lay and Clergy Views of Man's Original Nature, By Branch of Lutheranism

		By Percentage			
	Sample	LCA	ALC	MS	WS
A person at birth is neither good nor bad. (Disagreeing)	Lay ($p = .001$)	26	40	52	63
	Clergy ($p = .001$)	68	80	97	100
Man is naturally good but is taught evilness and wickedness in his environment and society. (Disagreeing)	Lay ($p = .001$)	34	38	48	53
	Clergy ($p = $ NS)	93	96	97	100
A child is already sinful at birth. (Agreeing)	Lay ($p = .001$)	50	64	82	84
	Clergy ($p = .001$)	83	87	99	100

2) "Man is naturally good, but is taught evilness and wickedness in his environment and society;" and 3) "A child is already sinful at birth." Each statement approaches the issue of man's nature slightly differently, but all attempt to measure the same aspect of the Lutheran ideological system. The LCA laymen and clergy take the most optimistic view of man's nature, and the WS laymen and clergy usually see man as naturally sinful (Table 7-1). In each branch the laymen more often than the clergy view man as good rather than sinful at birth. Such basic conceptions of human nature have obvious importance in analyzing human behavior and the ills of society.

The Images of Man Index

These three items formed an Images of Man Index.[1] Similar trends to those found previously among the four

TABLE 7-2
Lay and Clergy Rankings on the Images of Man Index,
By Branch of Lutheranism

Sample	Branch	Low	By Percentage Moderate	High
Lay ($p = .001$)	LCA	72	21	7
	ALC	58	25	17
	MS	40	27	33
	WS	34	24	42
Clergy ($p = .001$)	LCA	17	21	62
	ALC	10	12	78
	MS	0	6	94
	WS	0	0	100

Lutheran bodies and between the laymen and clergy appear in the index (Table 7-2). A high ranking indicates attitudes conforming with the traditional Lutheran doctrine of original sin. An individual's ranking on the Images of Man Index relates strongly to his degree of religious commitment on each dimension (Table 7-3). The theologically more conservative an individual and the greater his degree of religious commitment, the more likely he sees man as sinful by nature. Again the largest differences occur in connection with religious beliefs.

Analysis of the rankings by age shows a very unusual pattern. Older clergymen rank higher (more traditional)

on the index, but older laymen rank lower (Table 7-4). The clergy findings parallel previous results showing more conservative beliefs among older ministers, but the older laymen's optimistic view of man's nature is more difficult

TABLE 7-3
Clergy and Lay Rankings on the Images of Man Index,
By Type and Degree of Religious Commitment

Sample	Index	Ranking	Low	By Percentage Moderate	High
Clergy	Beliefs (*p* = .001)	Low	22	25	53
		Moderate	2	6	92
		High	0	2	98
Lay	Beliefs (*p* = .001)	Low	85	10	5
		Moderate	54	27	19
		High	21	32	47
Lay	Associational Involvement (*p* = .001)	Low	64	21	15
		Moderate	46	29	25
		High	42	25	33
Lay	Communal Involvement (*p* = .001)	Low	59	23	18
		Moderate	49	26	25
		High	41	25	34
Lay	Practices (*p* = .001)	Low	63	21	16
		Moderate	54	24	22
		High	37	28	35
Lay	Knowledge (*p* = .001)	Low	72	23	5
		Moderate	54	25	21
		High	33	25	42

to explain. Possibly a gradual wearing off of the religious teachings of childhood occurs.

A person's social class also relates to his ranking on the

TABLE 7-4
Laymen and Clergy Ranking High on the
Images of Man Index, By Age

Age	By Percentage Lay	Clergy
30 and under	33	76
31 — 40	27	78
41 — 50	22	86
51 — 60	23	87
61 and over	17	100
	$p = .05$	$p = .05$

Images of Man Index. The higher the class standing, the higher the ranking on the index. Fifteen percent of the lower, 27 percent of the middle, and 35 percent of the upper class Lutherans thus believe that man is sinful by nature. Suburban church members regard man as sinful by nature more than do members of inner-city churches. Thirteen percent of the inner-city laymen, 21 percent from outlying sections of the city, and 27 percent from suburban churches rank high on the Images of Man Index.

OPTIMISTIC AND PESSIMISTIC ORIENTATIONS OF LIFE

Viewing man as sinful by nature may cause Lutherans to take a pessimistic view of man and his potentials in the world. To measure this Lutherans were asked to agree or disagree with the statement "I believe that someday man may solve most of his problems on earth and live in a peaceful world." The majority of laymen choose a pessimistic

151

view, with 51 percent in the LCA, 58 percent in the ALC, 66 percent in the MS, and 70 percent in the WS disagreeing. Clergymen in all four Lutheran branches are even more pessimistic than the laymen, with 83 percent of the LCA and ALC, 94 percent of the MS, and 100 percent of the WS clergymen disagreeing. In almost every case the higher a clergymen or laymen ranks on an index of religious commitment, the more likely he disagrees that man can solve his problems on the earth (Table A-51).

If a relationship exists between a Lutheran's ranking on the Images of Man Index and his belief about man's capabilities for solving most future problems, one can conclude with some confidence that acceptance of the traditional Lutheran conception of man's basic nature has a strong bearing on an individual's convictions about man's potentials in the world. The data show that the higher a layman or clergyman ranks on the Images of Man Index, the more likely he disagrees that man may solve most of his problems and live in a peaceful world. Among laymen 50 percent ranking low on the index, 63 percent ranking moderate, and 84 percent ranking high disagree that man can solve his problems. For clergymen 52 percent ranking low, 79 percent ranking moderate, and 94 percent ranking high reject the view that man can solve problems on earth. Thus, the Lutheran ethic does seem to perpetuate a pessimistic view of man's potential.

GOD'S WILL VERSUS MAN'S WILL

Does the typical Lutheran think that God determines all his actions, and does he explain all events in terms of God's will or on the basis of a predetermined, God-directed plan? Does man make rational choices concerning his behavior for which he is going to be held accountable, both to God and to his fellow human beings? To what extent does a Lutheran feel that his actions and behavior actually work toward his own salvation? To examine these basic issues on

TABLE 7-5
*Lay and Clergy Views on God's Will Versus Man's Will,
By Branch of Lutheranism*

		By Percentage			
	Sample	LCA	ALC	MS	WS
When illness, injury, poverty, or bad luck strikes, it is the will of God. (Agreeing)	Lay ($p = .001$)	28	33	55	63
	Clergy ($p = .001$)	4	8	32	69
God has a predetermined plan for each of us on earth and there is little we can do about changing it. (Agreeing)	Lay ($p = .01$)	55	45	62	58
	Clergy ($p = .001$)	0	0	13	31
Man is created by God and subject essentially to His will. (Agreeing)	Lay ($p = .001$)	38	39	54	54
	Clergy ($p = .01$)	26	40	57	40
Man plays no part whatsoever in his own salvation or conversion. (Agreeing)	Lay ($p = .05$)	14	16	19	26
	Clergy ($p = .001$)	22	33	73	93

man's free will and God's will, Lutherans were asked to react to four statements (Table 7-5). On every question significant differences among the four Lutheran groups appear for both laymen and clergy. The MS and WS members more often see God as the dominant force governing all of man's actions, and the LCA generally stress greater autonomy for man in making decisions. Whether an individual sees God as totally in charge of his life, or whether he sees himself as essentially in control, will have an important bearing not only on his ideological outlook on the world, but also on the type of actions he takes in secular matters.

TABLE 7-6
Lay and Clergy Rankings on the God's Will Versus Man's Will Index,
By Branch of Lutheranism

Sample	Branch	Low	By Percentage Moderate	High
Lay (*p* = .001)	LCA	59	23	18
	ALC	59	20	21
	MS	36	30	34
	WS	34	30	36
Clergy (*p* = .001)	LCA	90	8	2
	ALC	78	22	0
	MS	37	42	21
	WS	40	13	47

God's Will Versus Man's Will Index

The four questions were combined to create a God's Will Versus Man's Will Index.[2] A high ranking stresses God's will over man's will, and a low ranking the reverse. Table 7-6 shows that the LCA and ALC Lutherans more frequently than MS and WS members say that man has a free will. This is particularly true of the LCA and ALC clergymen. Religious knowledge is the only aspect of religious commitment for which a high ranking does not correspond with a high ranking on the God's Will Versus Man's Will Index (Table 7-7). This suggests that the

Bible offers support for each of these points of view and that the Lutheran church teaches both.

Lutherans of higher social class emphasize man's freedom

TABLE 7-7
*Lay and Clergy Rankings on the God's Will Versus Man's Will Index,
By Type and Degree of Religious Commitment*

Sample	Index	Ranking	Low	*By Percentage* Moderate	High
Clergy	Beliefs ($p = .001$)	Low	89	11	0
		Moderate	63	31	6
		High	36	38	26
Lay	Beliefs ($p = .001$)	Low	68	18	14
		Moderate	46	27	27
		High	30	31	39
Lay	Associational Involvement ($p = .01$)	Low	54	22	24
		Moderate	45	29	26
		High	41	27	32
Lay	Communal Involvement ($p = .001$)	Low	54	26	20
		Moderate	47	26	27
		High	33	28	39
Lay	Practices ($p = .001$)	Low	58	22	20
		Moderate	46	28	26
		High	36	29	35
Lay	Knowledge ($p = $ NS)	Low	44	26	30
		Moderate	49	26	25
		High	46	25	29

The Lutheran Ethic

instead of God's will and power. Fifty-nine percent of the upper class rank low, 21 percent moderate, and 20 percent high on the index. A respondent's race also relates his views.

TABLE 7-8
*Lay and Clergy Views on the Means of Salvation,
By Branch of Lutheranism*

	Sample	By Percentage			
		LCA	ALC	MS	WS
*Man is saved by:					
Action and works	Lay ($p=$ NS)	17	18	9	10
God's grace		75	78	84	83
Man plays no part whatsoever in his own salvation or conversion. (Agreeing)	Lay ($p=.05$)	14	16	19	26
	Clergy ($p=.001$	22	33	73	93
People are saved by keeping the Ten Commandments. (Agreeing)	Lay ($p=.001$	60	59	54	46
	Clergy ($p=$ NS)	2	0	1	0

*Not asked of clergy.

While 47 percent of the white laymen rank low (man's will more dominant), only 18 percent of the Negro laymen do. Thus, white Lutherans place considerably more importance upon man's freedom than do Negro Lutherans. The emphasis on God's will among Negroes may partly explain the long period of Negro inactivity in the struggle for equality. Negroes traditionally have been religious fundamentalists.[3] However, Negro clergy leaders in the modern civil rights movement, such as Martin Luther King, Jr., have been theological liberals who stress man's freedom to change society rather than God's will.

MEANS OF SALVATION

The issue of God's will versus man's will relates closely to the question of how man is saved, or the means of salvation. Does man save himself by good works and/or proper behavior? Is God the sole determiner of who shall be saved and who shall be damned? Traditional Lutheranism teaches that an individual is saved by God's grace, through faith or trust in God. Man plays no part in his own salvation and is saved by faith alone (*sola fide*) .

Lutherans today show little consensus on the means of salvation. Laymen and clergy display wide variances, and there is little agreement even among clergymen. The first of three questions in Table 7-8 shows that the majority of laymen believe man is saved by God's grace, though the percentages giving this answer are far from unanimous.[4] Less than one in five of the LCA and ALC and about one in ten in the MS and WS believe that man is saved by action or works.

With the question on whether man plays a part in his own salvation the issue becomes even more confused. Traditional Lutheran teaching holds that man plays no part whatsoever in his own conversion or salvation. However, only a small minority of the laymen accept this idea, from 14 percent in the LCA to 26 percent in the WS. While there are only minor differences among the four lay groups, the proportion of clergymen agreeing with the statement varies greatly. Only 22 percent of the LCA and 33 percent of the ALC clergy agree, as compared to 73 percent of the MS and 93 percent of the WS.

The responses to the question on the Ten Commandments reveal definite problems between the clergy and laity in interpreting the Lutheran concept of salvation. More than half the laymen think that people are saved by keeping the Ten Commandments. In contrast, the clergy show great unanimity, with only 2 percent in the LCA, 1 percent in the MS, and none in the ALC and WS agreeing.

By the various aspects of religious commitment, the higher an individual ranks on each index, the more likely he is to say that man is saved by God's grace (Table 7-9). And one with a lower ranking on any of the indexes more likely believes that man is saved by action or works. Almost one-third of the laymen (29 percent) ranking low (theologically liberal) on the Religious Beliefs Index believe man can be saved by action or works. On the question of whether man plays a part in his own salvation or conversion, a similar trend appears for each index of religious commitment, except religious knowledge. The theologically more conservative and religiously more committed Lutheran more frequently see man as totally dependent upon God relative to life after death. The individual can do nothing to earn salvation. Such a theological position results in a deemphasis of good works, consistent with the Lutheran ethic.

Finally, a layman who ranks higher on any index is less likely to believe that people are saved by keeping the Ten Commandments. This is one of the few questions on which clergymen show no differences by theological stance. Age is a significant factor, and younger Lutherans more often see man as being saved by action and works, not by God's grace alone. They also more readily believe that man plays some part in his own salvation or conversion. In addition, younger Lutherans are less likely to think they will be saved by keeping the Ten Commandments.

A higher class standing for a layman corresponds with a belief that man is saved by action and works, that he does play a part in his own salvation, and that he is not saved by keeping the Ten Commandments.[5]

CONSEQUENCES OF LUTHERAN VIEWS OF MAN AND GOD

The Socialization of Children

What effect does a theology stressing an innate evilness of man, a pessimistic orientation toward life, a lack of individual freedom, and a means of salvation solely determined by God have upon values emphasized in the childrearing process? One would except as a result a childrearing philosophy emphasizing obedience. To investigate the possibility Lutherans were asked the question "If you had to choose, which thing would you pick as the most important for a child to learn to prepare himself for life? 1) to obey; 2) to think for himself; 3) to work hard; or 4) to help others when they need help."

Laymen from the theologically conservative bodies stress to obey, while those from liberal branches stress to think for himself (Table 7-10). The trend is accentuated among the clergy, with from 4 percent of the LCA clergy to 73 percent of the WS clergy selecting obedience alternative. Conversely, only 20 percent of the WS clergymen, as compared to 70 percent in the LCA, think it most important for a child to learn to think for himself. Thirty-five percent of the ALC clergy answer to help others when they need help, in contrast to 22 percent in the LCA, 19 percent in the MS, and only 7 percent in the WS.

An individual's religious beliefs, practices, and knowledge vary significantly with his views on childrearing. The higher one ranks on the beliefs and the practices indexes, the more he chooses to obey and the less to think for himself. The opposite pattern emerges for religious knowledge.

An older person more often stresses obedience. This is particularly true for the clergy. But the younger clergy are least likely to emphasize obedience of any lay or clergy age

TABLE 7-9

Lay and Clergy Views on the Means of Salvation, By Type and Degree of Religious Commitment

Sample	Index	Ranking	Man is saved by *			*By Percentage* Man plays no part whatsoever in his own salvation or conversion (Agreeing)	People are saved by keeping the Ten Commandments. (Agreeing)
			Action and works	God's grace			
Clergy	Beliefs	Low	—	—		21	2
		Moderate	—	—		47	0
		High	—	—		79 ($p = .001$)	1 ($p = $ NS)
Lay	Beliefs	Low	29	64		12	61
		Moderate	11	81		16	60
		High	3 ($p = .001$)	92		27 ($p = .01$)	42 ($p = .001$)
Lay	Associational Involvement	Low	23	67		12	65
		Moderate	9	84		18	57
		High	8 ($p = .001$)	89		26 ($p = .01$)	53 ($p = .001$)

*Not asked of clergy.

Lay	Communal Involvement	Low	18	74	15	61
		Moderate	12	83	20	52
		High	8 ($p = .05$)	84	24 ($p = .05$)	51 ($p = .05$)
Lay	Practices	Low	22	71	11	61
		Moderate	11	80	18	56
		High	7 ($p = .001$)	89	26 ($p = .01$)	47 ($p = .01$)
Lay	Knowledge	Low	19	65	20	76
		Moderate	15	81	11	56
		High	8 ($p = .01$)	89	26 ($p = .01$)	38 ($p = .001$)

*Not asked of clergy.

grouping. While none of the clergy age 30 or under choose to obey, 65 percent age 61 and over do.[6]

Social class is also a factor in values concerning child-

TABLE 7-10
Lay and Clergy Attitudes Toward Childrearing, By Branch of Lutheranism

Most Important for Child to Learn	Sample	By Percentage			
		LCA	ALC	MS	WS
To obey	Lay	17	20	27	31
	Clergy	4	19	33	73
To think for himself	Lay	66	64	58	52
	Clergy	70	44	38	20
To work hard	Lay	5	9	4	8
	Clergy	4	2	6	0
To help others when they need help	Lay	12	7	11	9
	Clergy	22	35	19	7

Lay — $p = .01$
Clergy — $p = .001$

rearing, and the lower an individual's class, the more he stresses obedience. Thirty-three percent of the lower, 21 percent of the middle, and 11 percent of the upper class Lutherans choose to obey as most important. Laymen reared in rural surroundings also emphasize obedience in children, with 18 percent of those reared in a large city, 21 percent in a medium-sized city, 25 percent in a small town, and 40 percent on a farm selecting obedience as most important.

Conflicts Between Science and Religion

A child reared by parents who stress obedience may differ markedly from a child brought up under a value system stressing independent thinking. One area where the effects of these childrearing philosophies often appear is opinions about science. Throughout history religious con-

TABLE 7-11
*Lay and Clergy Attitudes About Conflicts Between Science
and Religion, By Branch of Lutheranism*

		By Percentage			
	Sample	LCA	ALC	MS	WS
Conflicts between science and religion are "very serious" or "somewhat serious." (Agreeing)	Lay ($p = .001$)	43	46	58	63
	Clergy ($p = .001$)	17	32	53	69
A Lutheran can accept a view of the evolution of man from lower forms of animals as quite possible. (Disagreeing)	Lay ($p = .001$)	54	55	70	79
	Clergy ($p = .001$)	22	22	81	100

servatives have attacked science as a threat to the idea of a God-created universe. The theory of man's evolution from lower forms of animals has provoked especially strong criticism.

Two questions were asked of the Lutherans surveyed: "Would you say that conflicts and disagreements between science and religion are very serious, somewhat serious, or not very serious;" and an agree-disagree statement: "A Lutheran can accept a view of the evolution of man from lower forms of animals as quite possible." The data show large differences among Lutheran bodies (Table 7-11). In the theologically more conservative branches a majority of the laity and clergy often see the conflicts between science and religion as very serious or somewhat serious. The same is true for the question on biological evolution, with members from conservative branches usually disagreeing with the evolution of man. One hundred percent of the WS clergy, as compared to only 22 percent of the LCA and ALC, do not believe that man has evolved from lower forms of animals.

The theological stances of laymen and clergy show the most dramatic differences of any type of religious commitment on these two questions (Table A-54). For example, 6 percent of the clergy ranking low, 52 percent ranking moderate, and 95 percent ranking high (most conservative) on the Religious Beliefs Index disagree that man has evolved from lower forms of animals. In fact, the higher an individual ranks on any index of commitment, the more he opposes the concept of biological evolution. Finally, the higher a Lutheran's social class, the less likely he is to see serious conflicts between science and religion and the more likely he is to accept the idea of biological evolution.

Strict adherence to the Lutheran ethic, which suggests the rejection of the theory of evolution and the perception of conflicts between science and religion, may influence educational advancement and may discourage highly committed, conservative Lutherans from entering scientific professions. Consequently, Lutherans may be underrepresented in scientific fields, although no data is presented here to support this conclusion.

Economic Values and Occupational Choice

This study did not investigate the attitudes of Lutherans toward capitalism as an economic system or toward the prevailing occupational structure, but several writers have considered these issues. Weber and Troeltsch, in comparing Lutheran ideology to Calvinism, saw Lutheranism as less conducive to the rise of a competitive economic spirit.[7]

Certain occupations seemingly attract more Lutherans

than members of other denominations. Lazerwitz, for example, found that Lutherans were more likely to be farmers or skilled and semi-skilled workers and less likely to be found in the professionals, owners, managers, or officials.[8] In a Detroit-based study investigating the hypothesis that different religious preferences correspond with varying degrees of worldly success, Lutherans and individuals with no religious preference ranked ninth, below Jews, Eastern Orthodox, semi-Christians, Episcopalians, Calvinists, Protestants (no denomination), Methodists, and members of small sects. Only Catholics and Baptists were less oriented toward worldly success than the Lutherans.[9] Jonassen concluded from a study of Norway that unlike ascetic Protestantism, Lutheranism impeded industrialization because it lacked an ideology for a systematic rational ordering of the moral life.[10]

Finally, consistent with Lutheranism's traditional deemphasis of secular activities, Lutherans are underrepresented in politics. For example, although Lutherans were the fourth largest denomination in terms of members in the United States, they ranked eighth in the number of members in the Eighty-Seventh Congress.[11]

THE FUNCTION OF RELIGION

Lutherans have a conception of the function of religion that conforms with their ideological views of God and man. Theologically conservative Lutherans generally look to religion for salvation in the next world. In comparison, theological liberals more often see religion as providing moral standards for conduct. In any case, the large majority of all Lutherans say that they seek comfort and security from religion in handling the problems of their life.

Salvation Function

The responses to questions in Table 7-12 show significant differences among the four Lutheran bodies regarding the

TABLE 7-12
*Lay and Clergy Attitudes on the Salvation Function of Religion,
By Branch of Lutheranism*

		By Percentage			
	Sample	LCA	ALC	MS	WS
The most important thing is the salvation of mankind to eternal life rather than carrying on social reform programs here in this world. (Agreeing)	Lay ($p = .001$)	69	69	89	91
	Clergy ($p = .001$)	26	52	80	94
It is not as important to worry about life after death as about what one can do in this life. (Disagreeing)	Lay ($p = .001$)	35	38	55	63
	Clergy ($p = .001$)	26	37	71	94
Personal salvation is the chief reason for being a Christian. (Agreeing)	Lay ($p = .001$)	72	78	88	82
	Clergy ($p = .001$)	32	30	69	81

salvation function of religion. Laymen from the theologically conservative MS and WS emphasize the next world function of religion slightly more than those from the liberal LCA and ALC. However, clergymen from the LCA and ALC deemphasize the salvation function and put more emphasis on matters of this world.

On the assumption that the three questions tap similar attitudes a Salvation Index was developed from them.[12] Both laymen and clergy show significant differences by Lutheran branch (Table 7-13), with the theologically more conservative Lutherans more salvation or next world oriented (high ranking on the index).

Of the indexes of religious commitment, the Religious Beliefs Index reveals the most striking differences, although the higher an individual ranks on any index, the more likely

TABLE 7-13
Lay and Clergy Rankings on the Salvation Index,
By Branch of Lutheranism

Sample	Branch	Low	By Percentage Moderate	High
Lay (*p* = .001)	LCA	35	43	22
	ALC	30	47	23
	MS	13	42	45
	WS	12	40	48
Clergy (*p* = .001)	LCA	70	20	10
	ALC	66	19	15
	MS	22	28	50
	WS	0	31	69

he ranks high on the Salvation Index (Table A-55). On the beliefs index 88 percent of the theologically more liberal clergymen definitely are not salvation oriented. Although no differences appear among the laymen on the index with age controlled, large differences emerge for the clergy by age. Thus, while only 10 percent of the clergy age 30 and under rank high on the Salvation Index, 52 percent of the clergy age 61 and over rank high.

One's ranking on the index relates strongly to his attitudes on most other questions investigated. A layman or clergyman ranking high tends to take the most conservative stand on almost all the issues discussed. For example, the most salvation oriented Lutherans most often vote for conservative political candidates, oppose government social welfare, show most prejudice against Negroes, Jews, and Catholics, oppose social action within the church, take conservative stands on most moral issues, and oppose changes within the institution of religion. Thus, an individual's adherence to a this world or next world ideological orientation seems to be a crucial variable which affects his total life orientation.

Comfort and Security Function

In addition to being more salvation oriented, theologically conservative laymen more often see religion in this world as providing comfort and security. Females and older Lutherans also more frequently hold this view. Interviewers asked the laymen "Would you say you look to your religion more for 1) comfort and security in handling the problems of your life; 2) motivation to reform and improve our society; or 3) teachings and guides on how to behave?" The majority of laymen choose comfort and security in handling the problems they face in life, with the alternative selected by 65 percent of the LCA and ALC, 68 percent of the MS, and 77 percent of the WS. Laymen who choose for motivation to reform and improve society range from 13 percent in the LCA to only 4 percent in the WS. Finally, those looking for teachings and guides on how to behave range from 24 percent in the ALC, 21 percent in the LCA and MS, to 16 percent in the WS.

Opinions on what laymen seek from religion differ significantly by rankings on the Religious Beliefs, Associational Involvement, and Communal Involvement indexes (Table A-56). The higher ranking persons more likely are seeking comfort and security from their religion. An individual seeking comfort and security would be expected

to rank higher in associational and communal involvement.
Indeed, the church association and the Lutheran subcommunity probably meet part of the need for consolation.

TABLE 7-14
Lay and Clergy Attitudes on Moral Conduct, By Branch of Lutheranism

	Sample	By Percentage			
		LCA	ALC	MS	WS
The kind of life we lead or the way we behave will determine our future in the hereafter. (Agreeing)	Lay (*p* = .001)	82	78	69	60
	Clergy	*	*	*	*
The main purpose of the church is to help people live a good life. (Agreeing)	Lay (*p* = .001)	75	78	60	57
	Clergy (*p* = .05)	19	9	6	0
The most important thing about Jesus was that His life was an example of how people ought to live. (Agreeing)	Lay (*p* = .001)	79	72	67	53
	Clergy	*	*	*	*

*Not asked of clergy.

Women (75 percent) are more likely than men (60 percent) to emphasize this function. Also, the older members (over age 60—75 percent) more frequently seek comfort and security than the younger Lutherans (age 30 and under —63 percent).

Moral Conduct Function

The majority of laymen consider individual moral conduct to be an important part of their religious life (Table 7-14). However, individuals from the theologically liberal bodies are significantly more likely to stress moral conduct than those from conservative branches. Thus, contrary to

traditional Lutheran theology, LCA and ALC laymen emphasize personal behavior to the extent that four out of
every five individuals think that their behavior will deter-

TABLE 7-15
Lay Rankings on the Moral Conduct Index, By Branch of Lutheranism

Branch	Low	By Percentage Moderate	High
LCA	16	26	58
ALC	21	19	60
MS	32	24	44
WS	45	19	36

$p = .001$

mine their future in the hereafter. In contrast, clergymen
from all branches largely deemphasize personal behavior,
and only from zero to 19 percent see the main purpose of
the church as one of helping people to live a good life.

Since all three of these questions refer to the same function of religion, they were used to form an index of moral
conduct.[13] Laymen from the theologically more conservative MS and WS more frequently rank low on the Moral
Conduct Index and those of the more liberal LCA and ALC
rank higher, thus placing more importance on moral behavior (Table 7-15). The lower an individual ranks on
each index of religious commitment, whether in traditional
beliefs, associational involvement, practices, knowledge, or
communal involvement, the more he supports a religious
orientation with a greater emphasis on moral behavior.

Older Lutherans more often rank high on the Moral
Conduct Index, with 38 percent age 30 and under and 66
percent age 61 and over with this ranking.[14] An individual's
ranking on the Moral Conduct Index varies also with social

class, and the higher the class the less likely one ranks high
on the index. Sixty-two percent of the lower class, 45 percent
of the middle class, and 39 percent of the upper class Lutherans rank high.

TABLE 7-16
Lay Rankings on the Moral Conduct Index,
By Type and Degree of Religious Commitment

Index	Ranking	Low	By Percentage Moderate	High
Beliefs ($p = .001$)	Low	16	23	61
	Moderate	23	24	53
	High	46	18	36
Associational Involvement ($p = .001$)	Low	14	23	63
	Moderate	27	22	51
	High	43	21	36
Communal Involvement ($p = .01$)	Low	20	22	58
	Moderate	31	22	47
	High	35	23	42
Practices ($p = .001$)	Low	17	24	59
	Moderate	26	23	51
	High	41	19	40
Knowledge ($p = .001$)	Low	6	23	71
	Moderate	21	25	54
	High	50	19	31

The earlier findings on the attitudes about the church
and social action, and attitudes toward the church's becoming involved in secular affairs, support the conclusion that

The Lutheran Ethic

laymen's concern about moral conduct centers on personal, individualistic behavior. Moral problems to most laymen are those concerns specifically spelled out in the Bible, and laymen almost totally define them in terms of personal relationships and responsibilities. A concept of personal piety exists in Lutheranism, and the majority of Lutherans expect rewards in the next world for their moral behavior in this world.

VIII

Social Attitudes and Religious Ideologies of Major Denominations

THIS STUDY suggests that the Lutheran ethic encompasses a unique theological view of man, life, God, and religion. If it is a unique orientation, then we should be able to distinguish the ideology from other religious ideologies. Furthermore, we would except each religious orientation to have a measurable impact on the attitudes and values of its individual members. To investigate these possibilities we studied the social and religious attitudes of Roman Catholics, Jews, and non-Lutheran Protestants and members of the four branches of Lutheranism. The data were collected by questionnaires sent to a random sample of college students of all religious faiths attending a Detroit-area university (see Appendix I for details on sampling and methodology). The student findings cannot be compared directly with the data gathered in the general random sample of Lutheran laymen in the Detroit area. The primary value of the student information is the opportunity it gives to compare various religious ideologies to the Lutheran ethic and to measure their impact, if any, on secular attitudes and values.[1]

The student data offer further proof that the religious factor is important in analyzing behavior. A college student group is a rather homogeneous population and, consequently, any differences found among members of various religious bodies take on an even greater significance. The social characteristics of the students result in considerable built-in controls for social class and age.

The familiar trends among the four Lutheran bodies found in the lay and clergy samples emerge also in the student population. Whether on secular or religious issues, meaningful differences between members of the liberal and conservative Lutheran branches exist. In a number of cases differences are greater than those found among members of all other religious groups, including Roman Catholics and Jews.

Vast ideological differences exist between the Lutherans and the "liberal" Protestant bodies, the Catholics, and the Jews—differences reflected in social and religious attitudes. The students from the four liberal Protestant denominations studies (Episcopal, Presbyterian, United Church of Christ, and United Methodist) hold strikingly similar beliefs and attitudes. Surprisingly, Lutherans are as different from members of the liberal Protestant bodies as they are from the Catholics and Jews. Only with the Baptists do Lutherans show any similarity of attitudes, beliefs, and religious commitment.

Student members of all four Lutheran groups retain at least some characteristics of the Lutheran ethic, which distinguish them from the adherents of other religious faiths. The traits are most pronounced among students in the Wisconsin Synod. In contrast, the LCA members show the fewest characteristics corresponding to the Lutheran ethic. On a number of questions the attitudes of the LCA students correspond closely with those of members from the liberal Protestant bodies. The Jews, in comparison to the Lutherans, are very humanistically oriented, and they have much in common with the liberal Protestants. Catholics are oriented strongly to an ideology of "good works" and are very liberal in many of their religious and moral attitudes.

GENERAL ATTITUDES TOWARD RELIGION

On a series of questions used to measure the general attitudes of students toward religion, the WS members without exception show the most conservative attitudes (Table 8-1). For example, 83 percent of the WS students say they are still actively practicing the religion in which they were reared, 91 percent think that Scripture is the infallible authority for everything they believe and do, and 93 percent think that there will be a divine judgment after death. The LCA students are generally the most liberal Lutherans. The Baptists most closely approximate the attitudes of the Lutherans on almost every question.

Individuals from the four Protestant bodies (United Church of Christ, United Methodist, Episcopal, and Presbyterian) show a remarkable degree of consensus on the questions. Religion does not appear to play an important role in the lives of these students, with only about one out of four indicating that religion is very important in his life. Less than one-third say that they still actively practice the religion in which they were raised. While about seven out of ten say they believe in heaven or a life after death, only from 10 to 24 percent think that there will be a divine judgment.

Jewish students tend to hold similar attitudes toward religion as the members from the four liberal Protestant denominations, except that they much less often believe in heaven or life after death. In contrast to the Jews, however, where a little more than one-third say they still actively practice the religion in which they were raised, 70 percent of the Roman Catholics give such a response. In terms of

TABLE 8-1

Student Attitudes Toward Religion, By Religious Body

By Percentage

Question	Jewish	United Church of Christ	United Methodist	Episcopal	Presbyterian	Roman Catholic	Baptist	LCA	ALC	MS	WS
How would you rate the importance of religion to yourself? (Very important)	21	25	27	17	27	50	54	52	48	50	69
Are you still actively practicing the religion in which you were raised? (Yes)	39	29	26	27	29	70	47	41	69	54	83
Do you believe in "heaven" or a "life after death"? (Yes)	42	71	76	63	70	89	81	93	91	93	98
There will be a divine judgment after death where some will be rewarded and others punished. (Agree)	13	18	24	10	24	67	66	46	61	74	93
I believe that Scripture is the infallible authority and guide for everything we believe and do. (Agree)	16	18	22	17	25	35	52	30	48	59	91

the importance of Scripture the Roman Catholics more nearly approximate the liberal Protestant groups.

DIMENSIONS OF RELIGIOUS COMMITMENT

Religious Beliefs

Religious belief patterns similar to those appearing for general attitudes toward religion emerge (Table 8-2). In almost every case significant differences exist among the four Lutheran bodies, ranging from the most liberal beliefs in the LCA to the most conservative in the WS. Wider differences appear among the four Lutheran groups than among all other denominations, and the WS members give the theologically most conservative answers of any religious body.

The majority of the UCC students, United Methodists, Episcopalians, and Presbyterians reject traditional Christian teachings about the Bible, man, Jesus Christ, the devil, and the virgin birth. Jewish students hold beliefs paralleling individuals from the liberal Protestant bodies. In most cases Roman Catholics show only slightly more conservatism than the liberal Protestants and the Jews, even on the question relating to the virgin birth of Christ. The Baptists show great similarity to the middle-range Lutheran bodies (ALC and MS).

The first four questions in Table 8-2 were used to develop the Religious Beliefs Index,[2] which reveals that traditional Christian beliefs are strongest within the Baptist and Lutheran groups. Students from all other Protestant bodies rank as very liberal theologically. However, even within traditionally conservative Lutheranism, the LCA and ALC students give relatively liberal answers. Also, among student members the Missouri Synod no longer seems a stronghold

TABLE 8-2

Religious Beliefs of Students, By Religious Body

By Percentage

	Jewish	United Church of Christ	United Methodist	Episcopal	Presbyterian	Roman Catholic	Baptist	LCA	ALC	MS	WS
The Bible is God's word and all it says is true. (Agreeing)	9	17	4	0	4	13	40	11	32	43	74
The account of Adam and Eve falling into sinfulness is simply a story which did not take place in reality. (Disagreeing)	23	33	21	10	17	34	58	27	48	64	88
A child is already sinful at birth. (Agreeing)	2	3	4	2	5	23	30	48	46	54	83
Only those who believe in Jesus Christ as their Savior can go to heaven. (Agreeing)	*	13	11	6	10	4	57	35	24	48	77
I believe in the devil as an active and evil being in the world. (Agreeing)	5	8	10	2	5	36	47	30	33	44	71
It is possible for someone to reject the virgin birth of Christ and still be a good Christian. (Disagreeing)	25	29	23	14	23	27	53	31	31	47	72
A Christian or Jew can accept a view of the evolution of man from lower forms of animals as quite possible. (Disagreeing)	26	21	26	29	26	29	54	30	37	51	76

*Not asked of Jews.

178

of religious conservatism. For example, less than half (48 percent) of the Missouri Synod students see belief in Jesus Christ as Savior as necessary to get to heaven, and only

TABLE 8-3
Student Rankings on the Religious Beliefs Index, By Religious Body

Denomination	Low	By Percentage Moderate	High
United Church of Christ	87	13	0
United Methodist	92	7	1
Episcopal	100	0	0
Presbyterian	91	8	1
Roman Catholic	79	20	1
Baptist	47	28	25
LCA	60	40	0
ALC	59	34	7
MS	41	32	27
WS	38	33	29

slightly more than half (54 percent) see man as naturally sinful at birth.

On the Religious Beliefs Index (Table 8-3) Lutherans and Baptists are least likely to be theological liberals (ranking low). The LCA students are the most liberal Lutherans; with no members ranking high. Notably, while significant differences occur among the four Lutheran bodies, Lutherans of all branches have much in common when compared with other major denominations. Episcopalians, with all members ranking low on the index, are the most liberal denomination.

Associational Involvement

Students from the four liberal Protestant bodies (from 12 to 15 percent) are the least likely of any Christian group

TABLE 8-4
Student Rankings on the Associational Involvement Index,
By Religious Body

	Low	By Percentage Moderate	High
Jewish	72	26	2
United Church of Christ	62	32	6
United Methodist	64	27	9
Episcopal	61	32	7
Presbyterian	69	20	11
Roman Catholic	29	42	29
Baptist	45	24	31
LCA	57	21	22
ALC	42	33	25
MS	46	30	24
WS	38	33	29

to attend church once a week or more. In comparison, 41 percent of the Baptists attend this frequently. Lutherans range from 26 percent in the LCA, 35 percent in the ALC and MS, to 41 percent in the WS. Roman Catholics (68 percent) are most likely and Jews (4 percent) least likely to attend services at least once a week.

Another significant aspect of associational involvement is participation in church or synagogue activities and organizations, other than worship services. Students from the four liberal Protestant bodies participate less in church activities than the Baptists and Lutherans. Catholics and Jews parallel the liberal Protestants, although Jews (26 percent) are the least active of all groups. This question shows fewer differences among denominations than all the questions thus far analyzed, but differences still appear between the theologically liberal and conservative Protestant bodies.[3]

On the Associational Involvement Index, developed from these two questions, Jews are the least associationally involved, with only 2 percent ranking high (Table 8-4). Methodists, Episcopalians, Presbyterians, and UCC students have only slightly higher percentages. Only minor differences separate the four Lutheran groups in high rankings on the index, but large differences exist among those least associationally involved.

Religious Practices

The four liberal Protestant bodies and the Jews also have the lowest degrees of religious commitment, based on religious practices (Table 8-5). Not only are these students less likely to call upon God in making decisions, to try to convert nonbelievers to their faith, to ask for the forgiveness of their sins, or to pray, but they less often believe that their prayers are answered, and they more often view prayer as a psychological outlet for pent-up emotions rather than as a communication with God. Roman Catholics perform more religious practices than liberal Protestants or Jews, although they still fall considerably below the Baptists and Lutherans in most cases. The WS students have the highest percentages for every question.

The first three questions in Table 8-5 were used to form the Religious Practices Index. In every religious body, with

TABLE 8-5

Religious Practices of Students, By Religious Body

By Percentage

	Jewish	United Church of Christ	United Methodist	Episcopal	Presbyterian	Roman Catholic	Baptist	LCA	ALC	MS	WS
When you have decisions to make in your everyday life, do you ask yourself what God would want you to do? (Often)	5	13	11	12	11	18	30	16	20	27	36
How often are table prayers or grace said in your home? (At all meals)	4	8	18	7	13	16	32	15	28	32	42
Have you ever personally tried to convert a nonbeliever to your religious faith? (Many times or a few times)	9	12	20	12	11	26	47	33	36	46	48
How often do you ask forgiveness of your sins? (Very often)	7	9	13	5	14	26	28	30	33	34	50
How often do you pray? (At least once a day)	14	21	25	17	19	35	44	37	39	41	64
Do you feel your prayers are answered? (Yes, have no doubt)	16	33	29	10	22	26	44	30	43	49	60
Prayer is communication with God rather than just providing a psychological outlet for pent-up emotions. (Agreeing)	36	50	57	46	55	76	73	74	80	77	95

the exception of the MS and WS, more students rank low
than either moderate or high (Table 8-6). LCA members
rank low in about the same proportions as students from
the liberal Protestant bodies.

TABLE 8-6
Student Rankings on the Religious Practices Index, By Religious Body

	Low	By Percentage Moderate	High
Jews	84	14	2
United Church of Christ	74	26	0
United Methodist	60	33	7
Episcopal	73	22	5
Presbyterian	70	26	4
Roman Catholic	53	35	12
Baptist	41	27	32
LCA	68	12	20
ALC	45	38	17
MS	35	36	29
WS	31	27	42

Communal Involvement

The final index of religious commitment to be examined,
communal involvement, was developed from two questions.[4] The percentages of non-Lutheran Protestants who
say that their friends or relatives would try to discourage
them if they became a Catholic someday vary from 41 percent of the UCC students to 68 percent of the Baptists. The
Lutheran students show variances ranging from 48 percent
in the LCA, 60 percent in the ALC, 71 percent in the MS,

to 81 percent in the WS. Roman Catholics and Jews were not asked this question.

While the previous question investigates the potential

TABLE 8-7
Student Rankings on the Communal Involvement Index, By Religious Body

Denomination	Low	By Percentage Moderate	High
United Church of Christ	59	35	6
United Methodist	38	60	2
Episcopal	49	49	2
Presbyterian	39	56	5
Baptist	30	60	10
LCA	34	58	8
ALC	34	58	8
MS	27	58	15
WS	17	50	33

influence of an individual's religious subcommunity, another attempts to determine his desire to be influenced by the subcommunity. When asked if they would like to live in a community or subdivision entirely for people of their own religious faith, only from 3 to 11 percent of the non-Lutheran Protestants say yes. The Lutheran percentages are somewhat higher—11 percent in the ALC, 15 percent in the LCA, and 16 percent in the MS, and considerably higher for the WS respondents (36 percent). Six percent of the Catholics and 18 percent of the Jews answer yes. The Jewish percentage is large in comparison to most other groups, but it hardly provides empirical proof for the frequent assumption that most Jews prefer to live in a

Jewish ghetto. More interesting, however, is the fact that
the Jewish percentage is just slightly larger than the LCA
and MS totals, and just one-half of the WS percentage.
Thus, a significant minority of young Lutherans wish to
live in a religious ghetto, particularly those from the theologically most conservative WS.

The rankings of the various denominations and religious
groups on the Communal Involvement Index (Table 8-7)
indicate that more WS college students (33 percent) rank
high in communal involvement than WS members in lay
sample (26 percent). Thus, the next generation of WS
members and leaders show a slightly greater desire for subcommunal separation.

POLITICAL ATTITUDES

Although the majority of the students surveyed probably
had never voted in city, state, or national elections, differing political attitudes would still be expected to exist among
the members of the various denominations. As was shown
in Chapter Three, candidate preferences are one strong indication of an individual's political stance. The questionnaire asked whom the students would have preferred for
president in the 1960 election (Nixon or Kennedy) and in
the 1964 election (Goldwater or Johnson).

Differences among Protestant bodies in candidate preference in the 1964 election are small, and all nine Protestant
groups fall within a range of 32 to 46 percent preferring
Goldwater. Except in the ALC the Lutheran percentages
preferring Goldwater are slightly higher than in the other
Protestant bodies. In both the MS and WS nearly one-half
(46 percent) of the students preferred Goldwater; in contrast, only 22 percent of the Catholics and 21 percent of the
Jews selected him.

Among the non-Lutheran Protestants only small differences show up in the percentages preferring Nixon in 1960 (25 to 39 percent). The four Lutheran bodies have the

TABLE 8-8
Student Rankings on the Religious Sources of Anti-Semetism Index,
By Religious Body

	Low	By Percentage Moderate	High
United Church of Christ	84	16	0
United Methodist	81	15	4
Episcopal	86	11	3
Presbyterian	85	10	5
Roman Catholic	79	17	4
Baptist	53	30	17
LCA	60	32	8
ALC	75	23	2
MS	64	26	10
WS	43	31	26

highest percentages preferring Nixon—41 percent in the LCA, 43 percent in the ALC and MS, and 63 percent in the WS. The Roman Catholic and Jewish students preferring Nixon are 8 and 9 percent, respectively. The conclusion of a relationship between theological and political conservatism seems also valid among college students. The Baptist preferences for the two Republican candidates (25 and 34 percent) seem lower than their conservative theology might suggest, but the Southern Democratic tradition of many Baptist groups may account for this.

RELIGIOUS SOURCES OF ANTI-SEMITISM

The data in Chapter Four indicate that anti-Semitic attitudes may stem in part from religious theology itself. Similar results appear in the student sample (Table A-58). The
number of liberal Protestant and Catholic students who
agree with the statements suggesting religious sources of
anti-Semitism is quite small. On every question the Baptists
have the highest percentages among the non-Lutheran Protestant groups, and the Wisconsin Synod has the highest percentages of any denomination. More than one-third (36
percent) of the Wisconsin Synod students say they tend to
distrust a person who does not believe in Jesus. The WS and
Baptist students (17 percent and 26 percent, respectively)
rank highest on the Religious Source of Anti-Semitism
Index, while liberal Protestants and Catholics rank lowest
(Table 8-8). These data support the conclusion that conservative Christian theology contributes to anti-Semitism
in America.

MORALITY

The New Morality

College students are frequently regarded as proponents
and practitioners of the so-called new morality, and the data
reveal that they are indeed more liberal than adults and
clergymen. Nevertheless, individuals vary in attitudes by
denominational affiliation, with those belonging to theologically conservative groups less likely to endorse new
moral codes.

The respondents' answers to six questions, those used to
develop the New Morality Index plus three additional
items, reveal the greater moral liberalism among students

187

(Table 8-9). Approximately half the students indicate that premarital sex is all right for couples engaged to be married, with two-thirds of the Jews but only one-third of the Baptists and Wisconsin Synod Lutherans agreeing. The majority of students from the denominations disagree with the statement that serious emotional difficulties will result from premarital sex. Again the Jews are the most liberal and the Baptists and WS Lutherans the most conservative. Jews and Episcopalians have the most liberal and Missouri Synod Lutherans the most conservative views on extramarital sexual relations.

The New Morality Index indicates that students from all denominations take a comparatively liberal stand in regard to sexual behavior (Table A-59). More than half of the LCA Lutherans (52 percent), the ALC Lutherans (53 percent, the UCC students (56 percent), the Methodists (57 percent), the Presbyterians (60 percent), the Episcopalians (66 percent), and the Jews (71 percent) rank high (most liberal) on the index. In addition, the theologically most conservative Protestant bodies (MS, WS, and Baptists) have more than 40 percent of their members ranking high. Compared with Lutheran laymen in the Detroit sample, each group of Lutheran students has more than twice the percentage of members ranking high on the index. In the case of the WS, none of the clergy sample and 15 percent of the lay sample rank high, as compared with 45 percent of the students. Even among the Catholics, usually thought of as being especially conservative concerning sexual behavior, 47 percent of the students rank high in terms of new morality.

About nine out of ten of the liberal Protestants, Jews, and LCA Lutherans reject the idea that the new morality is "a device of Satan to undermine the consciousness of sin" (Table 8-9). In comparison, 50 percent of the WS students

TABLE 8-9
Student Responses to Questions on Morality, By Religious Body
By Percentage

	Jewish	United Church of Christ	United Methodist	Episcopal	Presbyterian	Roman Catholic	Baptist	LCA	ALC	MS	WS
It is all right for a person to engage in sexual relations before marriage with the person he or she intends to marry. (Agreeing)	66	59	50	46	58	42	35	59	44	46	37
Women who engage in premarital sexual relations are almost certain to have serious emotional difficulties. (Disagreeing)	81	79	79	80	77	70	63	67	68	69	59
It is possible that a particular situation could justify extra-marital relations. (Agreeing)	62	32	42	49	34	34	37	33	31	26	33
I look upon the "new morality" as a device of Satan to undermine the consciousness of sin. (Disagreeing)	89	88	89	93	88	82	57	89	76	79	50
Birth control pills should be made available to single girls of college age with no questions asked. (Agreeing)	72	50	39	61	57	42	35	48	39	36	29
In the area of sex relations, traditional religious standards are no longer adequate. (Agreeing)	83	79	72	73	67	67	44	59	56	55	33

express this view. On the item of whether birth control pills ought to be available to single girls of college age with no questions asked, only among the Episcopalians, Jews, and Presbyterians do more than half the students agree. The Lutherans again show their familiar liberal (LCA—48 percent) to conservative (WS—29 percent) trend. Forty-two percent of the Roman Catholics approve, despite the official Catholic opposition to artificial methods of birth control. Three of four Lutheran bodies have lesser proportions than the Catholics agreeing with the idea of making birth control pills available to single girls. On the question of whether traditional religious sex standards are no longer adequate, the Lutherans and Baptists most often say that they are and Jews (83 percent) that are not.

Abortion, Capital Punishment, and Drug Use

Individuals of varying religious backgrounds also express different attitudes and behavior regarding abortion, capital punishment, and the use of drugs (Table 8-10). The Lutherans (ALC, MS, and WS), Baptists, and Roman Catholics most often oppose abortion, while LCA students are least likely to oppose it.

On the question of capital punishment no large differences appear among any of the non-Lutheran bodies, including the Baptists, Catholics, and Jews, with from 32 to 46 per cent approving of capital punishment. Very distinct differences exist among the four Lutheran branches, with from 37 percent of the LCA to 64 percent of the WS students favoring capital punishment.

The rates of marijuana use among the students in the four Lutheran bodies is quite low, ranging from none to 4 percent. Highest rates exist among the Episcopalians (20 percent) and the Jews (22 percent).[5] On most of the moral-

TABLE 8-10

Student Views on Abortion, Capital Punishment, and the Use of Drugs, By Religious Body

By Percentage

	Jewish	United Church of Christ	United Methodist	Episcopal	Presbyterian	Roman Catholic	Baptist	LCA	ALC	MS	WS
A woman should have the right to get an abortion if she does not want to bring a child into the world. (Disagreeing)	35	34	42	28	38	64	47	26	56	46	55
It is right that convicted murderers should be given the death penalty. (Agreeing)	40	32	46	37	42	37	36	37	45	56	64
Have you ever smoked marijuana? (Yes)	22	0	6	20	10	7	4	4	0	4	2

ity questions analyzed the Episcopalian and Jewish groups generally have the most liberal attitudes. The finding on the use of marijuana suggest that the members of these same two religious bodies also exhibit the least traditional forms of behavior.

THE INSTITUTION OF RELIGION

Change Within Religion

In comparison to adults students generally are nontraditional in their attitudes. If religious ideology does have an effect on an individual's life orientation, however, one would still expect to find some differences among the various denominations on the question of religious change. Only 9 to 12 percent of the Roman Catholics and the students from the four liberal Protestant bodies think that maintaining the traditions of their religion is more important than changing forms, structures, and services to meet different times. Changes in Catholicism resulting from the Vatican Councils have strongly influenced the attitudes of young Catholics. The Baptists, Lutherans, and Jews more strongly desire to maintain religious traditions. Twenty-four percent of the Baptists, 28 percent of the Jews, and 54 percent of the WS Lutherans prefer to carry out the traditions of their religion the way they always have been. The WS students and the WS laymen and clergy most resist change within the church. Obviously, the desire to maintain pure and unchanging doctrine in the Wisconsin Synod has carried over into a rigidity of all religious forms.

On the possible change of a particular aspect of the religious belief system the students were asked to agree or disagree with the statement "Religious creeds can be expected to change over time." Of the Christian denominations the

Presbyterians are the least likely to disagree (16 percent) , probably a reflection of the recent adoption of the new Presbyterian creed. The four Lutheran bodies show large differences with from 30 percent of the LCA to 74 percent of the WS members disagreeing. About one-third of the Catholics and only 10 percent of the Jews oppose change.

The Role of Religion in the World

The most significant split among religious leaders today, often within as well as between denominations, involves the controversy over the ultimate role or purposes of religion. The dispute centers on a next world orientation versus a this world perspective. Lutheran students, compared to adult laymen, are not so traditional regarding the role of religion and look to the church more as an institution for reform of the conditions of this world. Ironically, however, students are less desirious of seeing the church issue statements on social, economic, or political questions. Thus, while they see religion as a force for social change, they still seem to adhere to the concept of separation of church and state. Not even one-third of the students in any denomination approves of church or synagogue leaders as a group taking a public stand on political issues (Table 8-11) . Except for the questions about taking a stand on social or political issues, the familiar differences exist among the four Lutheran branches. Individuals from the WS are the most conservative of all religious groups on every question. Jews are the most humanistically oriented, while the Baptists generally approximate the middle-range Lutherans in their views.

On the Social Action Index, developed from the first four questions in Table 8-11, the four liberal Protestant bodies and the Jews most frequently rank high, expressing attitudes favoring social action (Table 8-12) . Lutherans most

TABLE 8-11

Student Opinions on the Role of Religion in the World, By Religious Body

By Percentage

	Jewish	United Church of Christ	United Methodist	Episcopal	Presbyterian	Roman Catholic	Baptist	LCA	ALC	MS	WS
The church or synagogue can best contribute to the solution of social problems by preaching the Bible and winning individuals to salvation. (Disagreeing)	85	70	61	80	62	67	35	56	37	32	17
Religious denominations or groupings should issue policy statements on social and economic matters. (Agreeing)	31	49	41	35	41	37	35	27	35	32	17
The most important thing is the salvation of mankind to eternal life rather than carrying on a social reform program here in this world. (Disagreeing)	93	82	82	85	79	63	44	77	62	53	24
Church and synagogue leaders as a group should take a public stand on political issues. (Agreeing)	26	32	28	27	31	23	32	19	22	21	10
Rather than just preaching about sin, the church or synagogue ought to seek through organized social action to change the specific social conditions which produce sin. (Agreeing)	67	82	80	88	75	76	48	62	67	56	38

opposed to social action (ranking low) range from 12 percent in the LCA to 57 percent in the WS. Catholics least often rank high on the index (6 percent); however, two-thirds have a moderate ranking.

TABLE 8-12
Student Rankings on the Social Action Index, By Religious Body

	Low	By Percentage Moderate	High
Jewish	0	61	39
United Church of Christ	13	37	50
United Methodist	10	49	41
Episcopal	5	55	40
Presbyterian	9	51	40
Roman Catholic	27	67	6
Baptist	28	48	24
LCA	12	60	28
ALC	15	70	15
MS	34	41	25
WS	57	36	7

IMAGES OF MAN, GOD, AND RELIGION

Images of Man

Every religious ideology, either explicitly or implicitly, encompasses a basic image of man. The first four questions in Table 8-13 involve assumptions of man's original nature. The data show striking differences between Lutherans and the students from other denominations, with the exception

TABLE 8-13

Student Views of the Images of Man, By Religious Body

By Percentage

	Jewish	United Church of Christ	United Methodist	Episcopal	Presbyterian	Roman Catholic	Baptist	LCA	ALC	MS	WS
A person at birth is neither good nor bad. (Disagreeing)	17	18	22	13	11	28	41	31	43	54	74
Man is naturally good but is taught evilness and wickedness in his environment and society. (Disagreeing)	47	38	34	41	52	33	52	37	54	60	79
A child is already sinful at birth. (Agreeing)	5	3	6	7	11	38	36	48	52	70	90
Man by himself is incapable of anything but sin. (Agreeing)	7	8	11	10	6	13	42	33	37	47	57
I believe that someday man may solve most of his problems on earth and live in a peaceful world. (Disagreeing)	60	56	51	51	56	65	72	70	70	65	81

of the Baptists. Lutherans and Baptists more likely see man as naturally evil at birth. However, Lutherans themselves differ meaningfully on each question, with the LCA members least likely to accept the traditional concept of original sin. In most cases the WS percentages are approximately twice as large as those of the LCA students. The liberal Protestants, Jews, and Roman Catholics, compared with the Lutherans and Baptists, are very optimistic about man's original nature.

The last question in Table 8-13 investigates the possibility that an individual's view of man's nature affects his attitudes on the potentialities of man in everyday life. The Lutherans and Baptists generally disagree most with the view that man may solve most of his problems on earth and live in a peaceful world. Students from the four liberal Protestant groups are the most optimistic regarding man's problem-solving potentialities.

The Images of Man Index was constructed from the first three questions in Table 8-13. Approximately nine out of ten liberal Protestants and Jews, and three out of four Catholics, rank low on the index and thus take an optimistic view of man's nature (Table 8-14). Students most likely to view man as naturally sinful include the Baptists and Lutherans, particularly MS and WS members.

God's Will Versus Man's Will

Views regarding the extent of man's freedom in this world, and his freedom to save himself for the next world, may also vary from religion to religion. Some conceive of God as the cause of every event on earth. Two questions in Table 8-15 investigated these orientations. Less than one out of five of the liberal Protestants and Jews see God's will as dominating the life of man. The four Lutheran bodies

TABLE 8-14
Student Rankings on the Images of Man Index, By Religious Body

	Low	By Percentage Moderate	High
Jewish	88	12	0
United Church of Christ	94	6	0
United Methodist	91	7	2
Episcopal	90	10	0
Presbyterian	90	6	4
Roman Catholic	76	19	5
Baptist	62	16	22
LCA	58	27	15
ALC	52	29	19
MS	36	28	36
WS	12	31	57

show marked contrasts. Thus, while only 15 percent of the LCA students see illness, injury, or poverty as the will of God, 76 percent of the WS members express this view.

On the God's Will Versus Man's Will Index (Table A-60) the liberal Protestants, Roman Catholics, Jews, and the LCA Lutherans most often rank low, thus placing greater emphasis on man's freedom than God's will. However, vast differences emerge among the four Lutheran bodies, with only 26 percent of the WS students ranking low. They are more likely than any other group to see their total life as governed by God, and they place the least emphasis on man's freedom. Thus, the concept of man's lack of freedom prevalent in the Lutheran ethic appears to remain strong among young WS Lutherans.

The Means of Salvation

On the matter of salvation, a crucial aspect of religious ideology, members of all groups except the four Lutheran bodies and the Baptists most often believe that man is saved by "action and works" (Table 8-15). The Catholics (61 percent) have the largest percentage choosing this alternative. Only 23 percent of the LCA and ALC, 13 percent of the MS, and none of the WS students choose action and works.

Approximately 10 percent of the students from each denomination say that man is saved by devotion, with the Jews least likely to give this response (4 percent). The Episcopalians (22 percent) and the Jews (38 percent) in particular emphasize knowledge as the means of salvation; in contrast, none of the MS, and only 2 percent of the ALC and WS Lutherans give this answer. About one-quarter of those from the liberal Protestant bodies say that man is saved by God's grace, in marked contrast to the conservative Protestant groups, where 56 percent of the Baptists, 58 percent of the LCA, 59 percent of the ALC, 73 percent of the MS, and 85 percent of the WS students believe that God's grace is the central factor.

Salvation Function of Religion

Liberal Protestants and Jews largely deemphasize the salvation function of religion and show a strong this-world orientation. In contrast, Lutherans show wide variations with only a small portion of the LCA students oriented primarily toward the next world. As the Salvation Index shows, the WS members are the most likely of any group to emphasize the salvation function, with 34 percent ranking high on this index (Table 8-16). The ALC and MS Lutherans,

TABLE 8-15

Student Views on God's Will Versus Man's Will, By Religious Body

By Percentage

	Jewish	United Church of Christ	United Methodist	Episcopal	Presbyterian	Roman Catholic	Baptist	LCA	ALC	MS	WS
When illness, injury, poverty, or bad luck strikes, it is the will of God. (Agreeing)	16	18	15	7	19	34	32	15	43	45	76
"I see man as created by God and subject essentially to His will." (Agreeing)	9	9	13	3	18	17	26	15	24	35	69
How do you think man is saved?											
By action or works	49	56	50	42	57	61	23	23	23	13	0
By devotion	4	9	9	7	6	7	8	12	13	13	10
By knowledge	38	9	6	22	7	6	11	8	2	0	2
By God's grace	6	24	28	24	28	22	56	58	59	73	85

Baptists, and Catholics hold similar views, with from 16 to 21 percent ranking high.

TABLE 8-16
*Student Rankings on the Salvation Index, By Religious Body**

	Low	By Percentage Moderate	High
United Church of Christ	73	20	7
United Methodist	84	9	7
Episcopal	86	11	3
Presbyterian	79	17	4
Roman Catholic	56	28	16
Baptist	47	32	21
LCA	68	32	0
ALC	51	33	16
MS	51	33	16
WS	29	37	34

*One question used to develop index was not asked of Jews.

ECUMENICAL POTENTIAL

A significant number of mergers of various religious bodies, as well as increasing cooperative relationships through local, state, and national ecumenical organizations, have occurred in recent years. Many individuals applaud these movements, while others decry what they call the watering-down and compromising of traditional belief systems. As a measure of Protestant ecumenical potential, the students were asked if they tend to see all major American Protestant religions as equally good. Among the non-Lutheran Protestants 75 percent of the Presbyterians, 80 percent of the United Methodists, and 83 percent of the Episcopalians view all major Protestant religions as equally good. Among the branches of Lutheranism more than half of the LCA, ALC, and MS students give the same answer, indicating considerable ecumenical potential within Lutheranism. On the other hand, only 27 percent in the WS say the denominations are equally good.

In regard to non-Christian groups, only 11 percent of the Episcopalians agree with the statement that "only in Christianity is the one true God revealed." In contrast, 47 percent of the Baptists and 48 percent of the Catholics agree. The Lutheran percentages are higher (less ecumenical) than in most other denominations, with a range from 46 percent in the LCA to 85 percent in the WS.

Obviously, if individuals feel theirs is the only true religion, they will probably not want extensive denominational cooperation with other religious groups. On a final measure of ecumenical potential only 10 percent (Episcopalians) to 20 percent (Methodists) of the liberal Protestants in comparison to 37 percent of the Baptists say they feel disturbed about a watering-down of traditional beliefs in their religion today. The wide variation found among the Lutheran bodies probably reflects the ecumenical potential of these groups. Eleven percent of the LCA, 24 percent of the ALC, 34 percent of the MS, and 55 percent of the WS students say they are disturbed by a watering-down of traditional beliefs. Sixteen percent of the Catholics and 25 percent of the Jews also express such a viewpoint.

FINDINGS OF OTHER STUDIES

While the results of this study apply only to the population sampled, the data correspond with other studies showing differences in beliefs and attitudes among the various denominations. Stark and Glock found a similar continuum of denominations in their study of church members in Northern California and also in a national sample of adults.[6] As would be expected, the student responses are generally more liberal than those in the Stark and Glock sample, which included all age groups and social classes. However, the trends of differences among denominations are very similar.

Hadden's national sample of Protestant clergymen from six major denominations also showed a continuum corresponding to the one found for the students.[7] These results allow more confidence in the findings of the student sample.

IX

Conclusions: Trends in Lutheranism

ECUMENICAL POTENTIAL

THIS STUDY indicates that while Lutherans share similar beliefs and attitudes when compared with the members of other religious groups, important differences on many issues still separate both laymen and clergy in the various Lutheran bodies. Particular traditional issues demonstrate this dramatically and function to maintain the existing divisions within Lutheranism. In addition to large-scale disagreements on basic Christian beliefs, Lutherans show differences on such fundamentals as the role, nature, purpose, and function of the institution of religion.

Given these variances, what are the possibilities of extensive inter-Lutheran cooperation and ecumenical fellowship? The data indicate that the vast majority of laymen from all four Lutheran groups do not oppose allowing ministers from other Lutheran bodies to preach at their church, nor do they oppose open Communion among Lutherans (Table 9-1) . This is true even of about three of four laymen in the conservative Wisconsin Synod. In contrast, the clergy (except in the LCA and ALC) disagree extensively over these questions, with 98 percent of the LCA and ALC, as compared to none of the WS clergy, approving of pastors from other branches of Lutheranism preaching at their churches. A deep split among Missouri Synod clergyman emerges on the issue. The question of open Communion

TABLE 9-1
Issues Separating Lutherans

		By Percentage			
	Sample	LCA	ALC	MS	WS
Would you have any objection against a Lutheran minister from another branch of Lutheranism preaching at your church? (No)	Lay	100	99	93	78
	Clergy	98	98	47	0
Would you have any objection to a Lutheran from another branch of Lutheranism taking Communion at your church? (No)	Lay	100	97	88	70
	Clergy	100	98	76	7
A Lutheran can accept a view of the evolution of man from lower forms of animals as quite possible. (Disagreeing)	Lay	54	55	70	79
	Clergy	22	22	81	100
A person can be a member of a fraternal group such as a Masonic Lodge and still be a good Lutheran. (Disagreeing)	Lay	8	7	44	57
	Clergy	17	15	76	100

$p = .001$

reveals a similar pattern for both laymen and clergy, although three-quarters of the MS clergy express no objection to such practices among Lutherans.

Examples of particular issues that function to keep Lutherans apart are their views on biological evolution and membership in secret societies. Only the clergy in the LCA and ALC take a liberal stand on biological evolution. Members of the theologically conservative Lutheran bodies most often reject biological evolution as conflicting with actual Biblical accounts of the creation (see Genesis 1-3). This Biblical literalism, the belief that "the Bible is God's word and all it says is true," as opposed to the beliefs of more liberal Lutherans that the Bible does contain myths and errors, is the source of much of the division within Lutheranism.

The question of lodges and secret societies has had a long

TABLE 9-2

How Clergymen with Lodge Members Belonging to Their Church Are Attempting to Handle the Situation

Policy	By Percentage			
	LCA	ALC	MS	WS
Doing nothing, ignore it, see no problem, none of my business	81	59	18	0
Personal counseling, teaching, sermons	4	17	53	0
Just preach Gospel about Christ, salvation	6	14	16	0
Encourage more church involvement rather than lodge activities	9	10	5	0
Work to have them removed from membership, no Communion	0	0	8	100

and bitter history within Lutheranism. Theological conservatives believe that lodges, with their secret rituals, emit a religious philosophy of good works, which conflicts with the traditional Lutheran theology. Those who see conflicts between being a lodge member and being a good Lutheran range from 7 (ALC) to 57 percent (WS) of the laymen and from 15 (ALC) to 100 percent (WS) of the clergy (Table 9-1). Certainly little consensus exists except between the LCA and ALC. Significantly, the laymen in the MS and WS do not oppose lodges nearly as much as their clergymen do.

Ministers who say some members of their congregations belong to lodges—98 percent in the ALC, 91 percent in LCA, 37 percent in MS, and 6 percent in WS—were asked "How are you attempting to handle this at the present time?" Table 9-2 shows the different policy orientations among the Lutheran bodies.

The majority of the laymen from each body favor having all branches of Lutheranism merge (Table 9-3). However, most clergymen from the more conservative branches ex-

TABLE 9-3
Lay and Clergy Attitudes on Ecumenical Involvement

		By Percentage			
	Sample	LCA	ALC	MS	WS
Do you think it would be a good idea if all the various branches of Lutheranism merged? (Yes)	Lay	79	85	75	53
	Clergy	81	70	46	6
Do you believe that the Lutheran Church has the only correct interpretation of the Bible? (No)	Lay	86	80	65	46
	Clergy	89	89	48	13
Do you tend to see all American Protestant religions as equally good? (Yes)	Lay	72	71	55	44
	Clergy	60	28	10	0
Would you like to see your own denomination merge or join together with any Protestant group other than another Lutheran body? (Yes)	Lay	42	38	28	17
	Clergy	66	43	23	19

$p = .001$

press opposition. Only six percent of the WS and 46 percent of the MS clergy think merger is a good idea. If the members of a denomination view their religion as exemplifying the one true faith, then they will in all probability not desire merger or fellowship with individuals from other groups. A similar pattern to the answers given on the first question in Table 9-3 develops for this item also, with the LCA and ALC members more likely to believe that Lutheranism has no monopoly on the correct interpretation of the Bible.

Believing whether one's religion is the only true religion also has a bearing on whether Lutherans "tend to see all American Protestant religions as equally good." While 60 percent of the LCA clergy see little difference between American Protestant groups, only 10 percent of the MS and none of the WS clergy feel this way. The laymen in every branch more often than the clergy rate all Protestant religions as equal.

Finally, when asked "Would you like to see your own denomination merge or join together with any Protestant group other than another Lutheran body?" laymen, though much more likely than the clergy to view all Protestant groups equally, are not nearly as anxious to see their denomination join with another Protestant group. Only among the LCA clergy do a majority favor merger.

TOWARD HUMANISM AND THE DECLINE OF RELIGIOUS COMMITMENT

The data indicate that in Lutheranism a trend exists away from a belief system dominated by supernaturalism to one dominated by a humanistic orientation toward life. The foundations of traditional Christianity increasingly have been challenged, especially by clergymen. For example, only one in ten LCA and less than one in five ALC clergymen view the Bible as God's word and entirely true. More than three-quarters of the LCA and more than half of the ALC clergy indicate that belief in the virgin birth of Christ no longer is necessary to be a good Christian. Nearly a third of the LCA clergy say that belief in Jesus Christ as Savior is not essential to salvation. Finally, approximately half of the LCA, ALC, and MS clergy think that correct conduct more than correct belief indicates a religious man. Thus, the theological modernism which affected most other American Protestant bodies early in this century apparently has now permeated Lutheranism. The fact that the trends are strongest among the clergy, usually the defenders of the faith, is very significant for the future of Lutheranism.

Even members of the traditionally conservative MS show

little consensus on major beliefs. In fact, only among the WS clergy does any uniformity of beliefs exist, regardless of the age of the clergymen. In the other Lutheran groups

TABLE 9-4
Clergymen Ranking Liberal (Low) on the Religious Beliefs Index, By Age

Age	LCA	(N)	ALC	(N)	MS	(N)	WS	(N)
			By Percentage					
30 and under	100	(11)	40	(5)	31	(13)	0	(2)
31 — 40	61	(18)	69	(26)	11	(38)	0	(2)
41 — 50	44	(9)	42	(12)	4	(28)	0	(6)
51 — 60	25	(8)	17	(6)	10	(21)	0	(1)
61 and over	0	(3)	0	(2)	0	(10)	0	(5)

younger clergymen generally hold a theologically more liberal belief system than older clergymen (Table 9-4). This tendency is especially profound in the LCA, with none of the clergymen age 61 and over ranking liberal (low) on the Religious Beliefs Index, while all of the clergy age 30 and under rank liberal. Indications of change are also strong in the ALC, with the exception of the youngest age group (which includes only five cases). Change to liberal theology appears slight in the MS, but nevertheless a reality. Thus, while none of the MS clergy age 61 and over rank liberal on the Religious Beliefs Index, 31 percent age 30 and under rank liberal. A further indication of change in the MS can be seen when the percentages of clergymen ranking most conservative on the Religious Beliefs Index are analyzed by age. Although 90 percent of the ministers age 61 and over rank most conservative in their religious beliefs, only 31 age 30 and under have this ranking. The WS clergy show no signs whatsoever of theological change. Also, as Table

9-5 shows, lay members of all branches of Lutheranism show few, if any, signs of change (Table 9-5).

The LCA and to a considerable extent the ALC clergy-

TABLE 9-5
Laymen Ranking Liberal (Low) on the Religious Beliefs Index, By Age

Age	LCA	(N)	ALC	(N)	MS	(N)	WS	(N)
			By Percentage					
30 and under	43	(24)	36	(28)	18	(40)	4	(45)
31 — 40	48	(61)	28	(51)	8	(52)	16	(64)
41 — 50	55	(65)	23	(46)	16	(60)	3	(59)
51 — 60	40	(38)	34	(29)	17	(39)	9	(34)
61 and over	56	(51)	28	(33)	11	(30)	6	(25)

men appear to be moving with the liberal trend of American Protestantism.[1] The student data substantiates the tendency in the LCA. Also, the broad ecumenical activities of this body support the contention that "a loss of concern for traditional doctrine is a precondition for ecumenism, and thus that success of ecumenism today is a sign of the trend away from historical creeds."[2]

The religious beliefs of the ALC laymen and clergy are only slightly more conservative than those of the LCA, and the many years of close cooperation between the two groups may account for their similarities. Closer ties, perhaps even merger, are likely in the near future. The ALC also seems to be moving toward extensive ecumenical involvement with other non-Lutheran Protestant denominations. Finally, among both the LCA and ALC clergy a theology of social reform and humanism seems to be replacing the traditional Lutheran emphasis on providing comfort in this world and soul-saving for the next.

The MS, though still strongly theologically conservative, shows a trend toward change among young clergymen which probably cannot be reversed. Merger with the liberal branches of Lutheranism seems less than twenty years away. Very possibly the MS will be involved in a structural realignment within Lutheranism, resulting in the creation of two Lutheran bodies in America—one theologically liberal and one theologically conservative. The MS would probably be split in such a reorganization.

The Wisconsin Synod remains a strongly conservative Lutheran body, evidence that orthodoxy in Christianity is not dead. Neither laymen nor clergy give any indications of theological change. Compared to the other three Lutheran bodies, however, the Wisconsin Synod is a very small religious group and thus can more easily enforce its strict teachings. A fast rate of growth could produce circumstances similar to those now causing change in the Missouri Synod. Denominational growth often results in the acceptance of marginal members, such as through conversion at marriage, and here the seeds are planted for future liberalizing trends.

The Wisconsin Synod reveals three distinct features when compared to the other branches of Lutheranism. Its leaders agree on explicit goals for the church. Second, it has the greatest consensus among lay members on most issues and almost complete consensus among clergymen on belief issues. Third, the attitudes, values, and role expectations of the WS clergy correspond closely with those of their laymen.

With liberal theological beliefs comes a general corrosion of all forms of religious commitment.[3] For example, laymen from the theologically more liberal LCA and ALC rank lower in associational involvement, communal involvement, religious practices, and religious knowledge than laymen from the more conservative MS and WS. Members of the theologically more liberal branches also give less

financial support to the church, despite their higher average
yearly incomes (Table 9-6) . While the Missouri and Wisconsin synod lay groups each give an average of 53 cents

TABLE 9-6

*Comparison of Weekly Church Contributions with Annual Income,
By Branch of Lutheranism*

Branch	Median Annual Income	Median Weekly Contribution	Weekly Contribution per $1,000 Income
LCA	$10,527	$3.99	$ .38
ALC	10,308	3.99	.39
MS	9,942	5.30	.53
WS	9,845	5.22	.53

per week for every thousand dollars of income, the LCA
and ALC members give only 38 and 39 cents, respectively.

Regardless of particular denominational affiliation by
branch of Lutheranism, individuals holding theologically
more conservative beliefs emerge as more highly committed
in the other aspects of religious commitment (Table 9-7) .
Also, the theologically more conservative an individual, the
larger his weekly church contribution. Whereas the theologically liberal member gives an average of $3.88 per week,
the theologically conservative individual gives $5.75, de-
spite the fact that the conservatives have slightly lower
average incomes.

The institutional church may face serious problems as
the result of increased theological liberalism. The traditional forms of religious commitment, which are an important part of the ideology of theologically conservative
Christianity, begin to lose their importance as individuals
take more liberal theological positions. New religious philosophies with decreasing emphases on traditional types of

religious commitment may be developing. However, the institution of religion may become severely limited, or its own survival threatened, if financial contributions de-

TABLE 9-7
Comparison of Religious Beliefs and Other Aspects
of Religious Commitment

Ranking high on:	Ranking on Religious Beliefs Index, By Percentage		
	(Liberal) Low	Moderate	(Conservative) High
Associational Involvement Index	21	32	50
Communal Involvement Index	5	18	25
Religious Practices Index	17	34	51
Religious Knowledge Index	28	31	52
Median weekly church contribution	$3.88	$5.20	$5.75

crease. If religion becomes a privatized matter for individuals, then traditional religious institutions may cease to exist. A situation similiar to that in Western Europe may develop, where for 90 percent of the people institutional involvement does not exist. State support of the religious institutions, such as in Europe, is not beyond the realm of possibility in the United States. Indeed, the current pressures for government aid for parochial schools dramatizes the decreasing support of religion in the United States. The Gallup Poll shows that American people feel that religion is losing its influence in the United States, with 14 percent saying this in 1957 as compared to 70 percent in 1969. Younger adults (85 percent) more often hold this view.[4]

THE SCHISM BETWEEN LAYMEN AND CLERGY

Major belief and attitude differences exist between theologically liberal and conservative Lutheran clergymen. More important, however, is the growing gulf between the theologically liberal clergymen and the large majority of all Lutheran laymen. The new liberal theology centers on questions of reforming society, directly and immediately. In contrast, the traditional Christian objective involves saving the world by focusing on salvation of individual members of society. Theologically liberal clergymen want the institution of religion to challenge man to build a new type of world; most laymen look to the church for comfort and consolation. Hadden writes that the laymen "are essentially consumers rather than producers of the church's love and concern for the world, and the large majority deeply resent clergymen's efforts to remake the church."[5]

Within Lutheranism, clergymen with a theologically liberal belief system generally hold liberal attitudes on social issues. The pattern is very consistent and appears in connection with attitudes toward social welfare, foreign aid, war, race, anti-Semitism, civil liberties, abortion, the treatment of deviance, the new morality, women's rights, lay and clergy role expectations, social action, and civil disobedience. On all of these issues the stand of the theologically liberal clergymen is far more liberal than the vast majority of the laymen. In contrast to the clergy, lay attitudes frequently do not vary greatly according to theological stance. The social attitudes of the theologically most conservative clergymen closely parallel the social attitudes of most of the laymen. In terms of consensus on social attitudes, most Lutheran laymen would be best served by WS clergymen.

What distinctive elements exist in liberal Lutheran theology that may account for the wide differences between clergy and laymen? Particularly, what factors lead clergymen to see an urgent need for Christian social responsibility in challenging the existing order of the world, both by the individuals and by the church as a collective body? The liberal theology shows marked contrast to traditional Lutheran thinking, which has supported a deemphasis of worldly activity.

In contrast to the Lutheran ethic, theologically liberal clergymen more frequently take an optimistic view of man, stressing man's free will rather than God's will in determining human behavior. In addition, they usually believe that an individual is at least partly responsible for his own salvation or conversion. The liberal theology comes closer to a doctrine of justification by good works, in contrast to the traditional Lutheran emphasis on God's grace. The data support the contention that an individual moves (either consciously or subconsciously) from an emphasis on grace to good works as he moves from conservative to liberal theologically.

Other distinguishing characteristics of liberal Lutheran theology are evident. For example, liberal clergymen emphasize that a child learn to think for himself rather than to obey. They also see few serious conflicts between science and religion. They deemphasize salvation in the next world in favor of the church's role and the role of the individual in reforming this world. More than one-half (55 percent) of the theologically liberal clergymen say they are not concerned by, or look positively upon, the diminishing emphasis on supernaturalism in modern society. The strong desire for ecumenical activity with other Lutherans and Protestant bodies indicates a decreasing concern among liberal clergymen for doctrinal matters and an increasing concern for joint Christian efforts toward solving social problems.

A liberalization of theological beliefs seems necessary before Lutherans will become active in the world. The conservative Lutheran ethic inhibits social action, particularly collective action. The doctrine of man's sinfulness and evilness functions as a self-fulfilling prophecy, limiting social reform movements.[6] The function of challenging Lutherans to change society, to make it a "better" place to live, and the function of comforting Lutherans in a dynamically changing world, appear to be dichotomous.[7] Hadden comments on the laymen's view of the church:

> Their church may be largely confined to four walls, their friends, and a salaried comforter, but it is a church they want and need. For them, the church is not an agent of change, but rather a buffer against it. They do not understand what clergy are saying and doing, nor are they willing to lend consent on the assumption that clergy understand better than they the "will of God." The result is that clergy and laity are on a collision course. In a very real sense the laity have one church and the clergy have another.[8]

Currently Lutheran ministers, when compared to clergymen from other Protestant bodies, are among the least likely to engage in social action and protest movements, although many activist Lutheran clergymen have participated in particular social reform struggles.[9] However, with Lutheran clergymen becoming increasingly theologically liberal, more massive involvement can be expected. LCA and ALC clergymen thus far have been the most active, although particular MS clergymen also have participated in social action movements. The WS clergy and the large majority of the more conservative MS clergy remain uninvolved and, consequently, in harmony with the attitudes and desires of most laymen.

The theologically liberal clergymen face crucial personal dilemmas. Spurred with a passionate, emotional desire to act, they often lack a complete understanding of the problems they deal with. Their liberal colleagues pressure them to stand up and be counted, while local parishes or denominational leaders threaten them with strong sanctions if they do. The liberal clergyman experiences considerable frustration in his vocation. Clergy responses to the question "Have you ever considered leaving the ministry for some other vocation?" reveal this more clearly. Thirty-six percent of the liberal ministers say they have thought very seriously of leaving the ministry, and another 24 percent have considered it. By far the largest proportion of clergymen who have contemplated leaving the ministry are in the LCA and ALC. No WS clergyman says he has ever thought seriously of leaving the ministry.[10]

A potential crisis between theologically liberal Lutheran clergy and most lay members seems in its early stages. The bases for this schism already appear, and a more intense struggle seems ahead. The confrontation will be crucially important for the future of Lutheranism and Christianity.

A NEW APPROACH TO SOCIOLOGICAL STUDY OF RELIGION

This investigation of Lutheranism illustrates a theoretical perspective for studying religion from the sociological point of view. The disadvantages of lumping all Protestants, Catholics, and Jews into a single category, as in most previous studies, should now be obvious. Studying religion by denominational groups seems to be only a minor improvement. To speak of *the* Lutheran theological point of view, for example, is as meaningless as reading the opinions of

"Lutherans" in a Gallup Poll. It is just as meaningless to speak of Baptists, Presbyterians, or Episcopalians in terms of lump-sum percentages. Apparently as much, if not more, variation exists within these religious bodies as between them. Thus a new theoretical formulation to analyze religion in America is needed.

Religious ideology exists in all societies because it supplies answers to certain important questions for man. Religion provides a meaning for life and death and an explanation for sickness, injustice, and suffering. It also explains why evil exists and why man faces frustrations, providing answers to questions he cannot find elsewhere. Talcott Parsons suggests that "man's knowledge of the empirical world, and the expectations oriented to and by his knowledge, cannot alone constitute adequate mechanisms of adjustment." Religious belief systems, he indicates, handle discrepancies between expectations in terms of the institutionalized value system in society and the actual course of events. This occurs in two primary ways. One approach may be called "compensatory re-equilibration." According to this view "unmerited good fortune and undeserved suffering will be compensated somewhere." Through this means, "sources of strain involved in 'meaningless' discrepancies between what the institutionized system through its ideology says ought to happen to people, and what in fact does, are ironed out."[11] The focus here is on another world after physical death which far transcends the problems of life. The second ideological approach to man's frustrations, "progressive orientation," focuses on the social reformation of this world. Individuals seek compensation for discrepancies through improvement of the social system rather than in the transcendental sphere.

These two ideological commitments have much in common with the familiar designations of theological conservatism and liberalism. Religion provides these two basic ideological systems, which penetrate into all areas of life. Usually one or the other will dominate in a particular religious group. When both exist within the same group or denomination, this usually indicates that change is taking place. The ideologies theoretically are mutually exclusive, and they usually conflict. An individual generally focuses his total life organization in accordance with one of these orientations, depending, of course, upon his degree of religious commitment. Outlined below are some of the polar characteristics of belief and value systems related to the two ideologies.

Theological Liberalism *(Progressive Orientation)*	*Theological Conservatism* *(Compensatory Re-equilibration)*
Nonliteral interpretation of the Bible	Literal interpretation of the Bible
This world orientation, emphasizing social reform	Next world orientation, emphasizing salvation
Events explained by human causes	Events explained as the will of God
Clergymen viewed as ethical and prophetic leaders	Clergymen viewed as spiritual leaders and servants
Stress of intellectual independence	Stress of obedience to authority
Relative or situational standards of morality	Absolute standards of morality
Opposition to harsh methods of punishing deviants	Recommendation of harsh methods of punishing deviants

Changing religious creeds, doctrines and beliefs	Nonchanging religious creeds, doctrines, and beliefs
Positive attitudes toward science	Negative attitudes toward science
Equalitarian role for women	Subservient role for women
Strong ecumenical orientation	Function in terms of religious isolation
Desire for heterogeneous relationships	Strong communal orientation
Social activism	Social quietism, passivity
Tolerant attitudes toward minorities and in granting civil liberties	Intolerant attitudes toward minorities and in granting civil liberties
Stress of group action	Stress of religious individualism
Political liberalism	Political conservatism
Deemphasis of individual responsibility and support of government welfare	Stress of individual responsibility and oppose government welfare

The two ideological systems, and each item within the system, form opposite poles on a continuum, one emphasizing religion as a force for change and the other emphasizing religion as a force for maintaining the status quo. Each represents a set of consistent attitudes toward man, God, and the world.

The data gathered in this study provide an opportunity to test this approach to the study of religion. Questions relating to the seventeen characteristics listed were included.[12] The analysis shows that most clergymen take a stand on issues in a consistently liberal or consistently conservative manner, demonstrating the usefulness of studying religion from this point of view.

TABLE 9-8
Liberal-Conservative Views on Issues for Clergymen with Liberal or Conservative Ideological Systems, By Branch of Lutheranism

	Theologically Liberal		Theologically Conservative	
	N	Liberal Answers (By Percentage)	N	Conservative Answers (By Percentage)
LCA	48	91	6	68
ALC	40	80	12	71
MS	25	76	91	84
WS	0	—	16	99
Totals	113	84	125	84

The clergymen in the four branches of Lutheranism usually lean toward either a liberal or a conservative ideological system and have been grouped accordingly (Table 9-8). The clergymen who tend toward theological liberalism give liberal answers to 84 percent of various issues. Similarly, of the clergymen who lean toward a conservative world view, 84 percent give conservative responses. This suggests that most individuals show a high degree of consistency of values in their total life organization.

The most liberal LCA and most conservative WS Lutheran bodies have the highest degree of consistency of values among their clergymen. For example, all WS clergymen hold to a conservative life orientation, and they give conservative responses to 99 percent of all the issues. Among the LCA clergymen the opposite pattern emerges, and forty-eight out of fifty-four clergymen hold liberal belief systems.

Those who are on the liberal side of the continuum answer, on the average, 91 percent of all the issues with liberal answers. Both the ALC and MS show more severe splits, but even among these clergymen an individual answers most of the questions with relatively consistent liberal or conservative responses.

These two basic ideological systems are derived from Lutheranism, but the same ideal-type orientations likely also hold true for Protestantism generally. With slight modifications the same theoretical model may apply to other major religions. In any case, the study of religion with a focus on total ideological stance across denominational lines affords exciting prospects for future research.

Notes

Chapter I

1. Theoretical discussions and research studies relating to Weber's Protestant Ethic thesis include the following: R. H. Tawney, *Religion and the Rise of Capitalism: A Historical Study* (New York, 1926); Werner Sombart, *The Jews and Modern Capitalism,* trans. M. Epstein (London, 1913); Ernst Troeltsch, *The Social Teaching of the Christian Churches,* trans. Olive Wyon (New York, 1931), II; Gerhard Lenski, *The Religious Factor: A Sociological Study of Religion's Impact on Politics, Economics, and Family Life* (New York, 1961); Albert Mayer and Harry Sharp, "Religious Preference and Wordly Success," *American Sociological Review,* XXVII (April 1962), 218-27; Helmut R. Wagner, Kathryn Doyle, and Victor Fisher, "Religious Background and Higher Education," *American Sociological Review,* XXIV (December 1959), 852-56; Christen T. Jonassen, "The Protestant Ethic and the Spirit of Capitalism in Norway," *American Sociological Review,* XII (1947), 676-86; Andrew M. Greeley, "The Protestant Ethic: Time for a Moratorium," *Sociological Analysis,* XXV (1964), 20-33; Richard L. Means, "American Protestantism and Max Weber's Protestant Ethic," *Religious Education,* LX (1965), 90-98.

2. *The Book of Concord: The Confessions of the Evangelical Lutheran Church,* trans. and ed. Theodore G. Tappert *et al.* (Philadelphia, 1959), p. 510.

3. Martin Luther, *Martin Luther: Selections From His Writings,* ed. John Dillenberger (Garden City, N. Y., 1961), p. 203.

4. *The Book of Concord,* p. 225.

5. Martin Luther, quoted in Erich Fromm, *Escape from Freedom* (New York, 1941), p. 75.

6. *The Protestant Ethic and the Spirit of Capitalism,* trans. Talcott Parsons (New York, 1958), p. 102. The original work was published in the form of two articles in 1904 and 1905.

7. *Ibid.,* p. 112.
8. Troeltsch, pp. 534-35.
9. *Ibid.,* pp. 563, 576.
10. Martin Luther, quoted in H. Richard Niebuhr, *Christ and Culture* (New York, 1951), pp. 171-72.
11. Weber, pp. 81, 85.
12. Troeltsch, p. 563.
13. Luther, quoted in Fromm, p. 82.
14. Troeltsch, p. 560.
15. p. 95.
16. p. 543.
17. p. 89.
18. pp. 555, 561.
19. Martin Luther, quoted in Tawney, pp. 93-94.
20. p. 171.
21. p. 128.
22. p. 188.

Chapter II

1. Charles Y. Glock, "On the Study of Religious Commitment," Survey Research Center, University of California, Berkeley, reprinted from *Religious Education* LVII (July-August 1962); Charles Y. Glock, Benjamin E. Ringer, and Earl R. Babbie, *To Comfort and to Challenge* (Berkeley, 1967), Charles Y. Glock and Rodney Stark, *Religion and Society in Tension* (Chicago, 1965); Rodney Stark and Charles Y. Glock, *American Piety: The Nature of Religious Commitment* (Berkeley, 1968); Yoshio Fukuyama, "The Major Dimensions of Church Membership," *Review of Religious Research,* II (Spring 1961), pp. 154-61: Fukuyama, *Styles of Church Membership* (New York, 1961) (Mimeographed); Joseph H. Fichter, *Social Relations in the Urban Parish* (Chicago, 1954); and Lenski, *The Religious Factor.*

2. For a summary of the methodology utilized in collecting these samples see Appendix I.

3. The level of significance (*p*) is a measure of the reliability of the differences found between two or more percentages. If the differences are not statistically significant (NS) then they could well have occurred simply by chance. A significance level of .05 indicates that the differences in the percentages could have occurred by chance only five times in one hundred. Similarly, with a significance level of .01 the differences could have occurred by chance only one time in one hundred and with a level of .001 only one time in one thousand. Thus, as one moves from the .05 to the .001 level of significance, greater confidence can be placed in the findings.

4. Clergymen were also ranked in terms of beliefs on the basis of their stated theological position, rating themselves as: fundamentalist, conserva-

tive, neo-orthodox, moderate, liberal, radical, or other. An extremely high correlation resulted between a clergymen's self-ranking and his ranking on the Religious Beliefs Index. Clergymen appear to have an accurate self-assessment of their theological stance in comparison with their fellow clergymen.

5. Jeffrey K. Hadden, *The Gathering Storm in the Churches: The Widening Gap Between Clergy and Laymen* (New York, 1969). Differences in the types of responses allowed, and in the wording of the questions themselves, make comparisons somewhat difficult between the two studies. Hadden uses a six-point continuum in his studies compared to the four-point continuum in the present study.

6. *American Piety*.

7. For complete tables on all social correlates the reader is referred to the following manuscript on microfilm: Lawrence Kersten, "The Lutheran Ethic and Social Change" (unpublished Ph.D. dissertation, Department of Anthropology and Sociology, Wayne State University, 1968). Copies available through University Microfilms, Ann Arbor, Mich.

8. A respondent's social class was determined by the number of total points he received for his level of income and education. The range of income and educational levels, and the points given for each level, were as follows: *income,* under $6,000—zero points; $6,000 to $11,999—one point; $12,000 and over—two points. For *education,* less than high school—zero points; finished high school—one point; at least some college—two points. When the income and educational scores were added, the most points an individual could receive was 4, while the least was zero. Respondents with a score of 4 were classified upper class, 2 or 3 middle class, and 0 or 1 lower class.

9. While data comparing Lutherans who have attended parochial schools with those who have attended public schools only was collected in this study, it is not extensively analyzed in this volume. The only meaningful differences between these two groups were found in relation to three of the dimensions of religious commitment; that is, in terms of religious beliefs, religious practices, and religious knowledge. There was no evidence of any differences on any of the questions relating to secular attitudes. It appears that the parochial school, functioning as most secondary groups do, has very little effect on an individual's attitudes and values outside of the institution of religion. Moreover, caution must even be exercised in attributing the religious differences that were found to the parochial school system, since family background may be the crucial underlying variable.

10. Inner-city churches were those located within the boundaries of Livernois, Six Mile Road, and Conner. A second geographical designation including all those churches in the outlying sections of the central city of

Detroit—excluding those in the inner city. Suburban churches included those outside the boundaries of the city of Detroit, except for Highland Park and Hamtramck.

11. In developing the Associational Involvement Index one point was given to Lutherans attending church once a week or more, and one point to those answering yes to the question dealing with other types of institutional involvement. As a result, the scores for the laymen range from a minimum of 0 to a high of 2. The score of 0 was ranked low, 1 was moderate, and 2 was high. Validation is assumed on the basis of face validity.

12. A respondent was given one point on the first question if he said he called upon God often in making decisions. One point was given in the second question if table prayers were said at all meals. Finally, one point was given if the individual had tried to convert a nonbeliever many times or a few times. The resulting scores ranged from 0 to 3, with 0 ranked low, 1 moderate, and 2 or 3 high. For validity see Table A-8.

13. The religious knowledge questions were not designed as a test or measurement of the overall level of religious knowledge. Pretests showed that the general level of knowledge was so low that many knowledge questions had to be discarded because only a few persons interviewed could give the correct answers. It was our purpose to build a Religious Knowledge Index measuring all individuals, from the most knowledgeable to the least knowledgeable. To accomplish this some assurance was necessary that a fairly large percentage of the respondents would get at least some correct answers. Thus, the easiest questions of the thirty or so utilized in the pretests were included in the final interview schedule. Local clergymen agreed that they represented a minimal level of religious knowledge. The reader who is interested in the exact results of the questions by branch of Lutheranism is referred to the author's dissertation manuscript.

14. Total scores ranged from 0 to 9. Respondents with scores of 0, 1, or 2 were ranked low, scores of 3, 4, or 5 were ranked moderate, and 6 to 9 were ranked high. Validation was assumed on the basis of face validity.

15. The question can justifiably be raised as to whether this index, which is based entirely on Biblical questions, is also reflective of other more general kinds of religious knowledge. When other types of religious knowledge questions were analyzed, the index seemed to be a good predictor of how the individuals answer non-Biblical religious knowledge questions. For example, 7 percent ranked low, 16 percent moderate, and 31 percent high on the Religious Knowledge Index correctly named the president of their Lutheran denomination. Also, those who chose the correct century in which Martin Luther lived included 22 percent ranked low, 36 percent moderate, and 63 percent high on the knowledge index.

16. A respondent was given one point if he answered would try to the question relating to his friends and relatives trying to discourage him from becoming a Catholic. One point was also given if he answered yes to desiring

to live in a Lutheran community or subdivision. Total scores ranged from 0 to 2 with 0 ranked low, 1 moderate, and 2 high.

17. To test the validity of the Communal Involvement Index we compared to see whether answers to six other questions could be predicted on the basis of an individual's ranking on the index (Table A-14). The results are as would be expected if the index is measuring communal involvement accurately. A person ranking high in communal involvement is nearly three times as likely as a person ranking low to associate mostly with other Lutherans in everyday affairs (35 percent versus 12 percent). Similarly, an individual ranking high on the index is considerably more likely than a person ranking low to choose Lutherans as his three or four closest friends (49 percent versus 18 percent). In addition, the person ranking high more likely comes from a family where most of his relatives are Lutherans (75 percent versus 44 percent). Such a person is also most likely to have been a Lutheran from childhood, never having belonged to another denomination. Finally, those ranking high are significantly more likely to favor their denomination's providing parochial elementary and high schools.

18. The Pearson Product Moment Correlation was used as the measure of correlation. Correlation is a statistical tool for measuring the amount and direction of related variation between two variables. Its measurements range from $r = +1.00$ (perfect positive correlation in which each measured variable varies one unit in the same direction for each unit of variation of the other variable) through $r = 0$ (no correlation, or no related variation among measured variables) to $r = -1.00$ (perfect negative correlation in which each measured variable varies one unit in the opposite direction for each unit of variation of the other variable).

19. See Lenski, pp. 2, 24; Fukuyama, p. 159; and Stark and Glock, pp. 174-82.

Chapter III

1. For example, Paul Lazarfeld, Bernard Berelson, and Hazel Caudet, *The Peoples' Choice* (New York, 1948); *The Religious Factor;* Oscar Gantz, "Protestant and Catholic Voting Behavior in a Metropolitan Area," *Public Opinion Quarterly,* XXIII (Spring 1959); Angus Campbell and associates, *The American Voter* (New York, 1960).

2. Benton Johnson, "Ascetic Protestantism and Political Preference," *Public Opinion Quarterly,* XXVI (Spring 1962), pp. 35-46; "Ascetic Protestantism and Political Preference in the Deep South," *American Journal of Sociology,* LXIX (January 1964), pp. 359-65; "Theology and Party Preference Among Protestant Clergymen," *American Sociological Review,* XXXI (April 1966), pp. 200-208; Hadden, *The Gathering Storm in the Churches.*

3. Johnson, "Protestant Clergymen," p. 201.

4. Hadden, p. 73.

The Lutheran Ethic

5. Scoring: one point for each answer favoring government action in social welfare (liberal responses are in parentheses at the end of each question in Table 3-7). Possible scores ranged from zero to 4. Respondents with scores of 0 or 1 were ranked low, 2 were ranked moderate, and 3 or 4 were ranked high. For validation, see Table A-20.

6. Similar results were found by Harold E. Quinley, "Hawks and Doves Among the Clergy: Protestant Reactions to the War in Vietnam," *Ministry Studies, III* (October 1969), 5-18.

Chapter IV

1. American Institute of Public Opinion, *Gallup Opinion Index—Special Report on Religion* (Princeton, 1967), pp. 17-23. Nonwhite members of major denominations include 24 percent of the Baptists, 9 percent of the Methodists, 6 percent of the Episcopalians, 5 percent of the Roman Catholics, 2 percent of the Presbyterians, and 1 percent of the Lutherans.

2. The lay interviews including these questions were completed a few months before the Detroit riot in the summer of 1967. Until that time Detroit had been considered to have one of the best records in race relations of any major metropolitan area in the United States. It is possible that more negative feelings toward Negroes would have been found had the interviews been conducted after the riot.

3. Scoring: one point for each answer that suggested prejudice toward Negroes. Range: 0 to 5, with 0 classified as low, 1 or 2 moderate, and 3, 4, or 5 high. For validation, see Table A-23.

4. Lenski, *The Religious Factor,* p. 295.

5. Scoring one point for each answer that inferred distrust or prejudice toward Jews. Range: 0 to 3, with a score of 0 ranking low, 1 moderate, and 2 or 3 high. Logical validation or face validity was assumed.

6. Lenski, pp. 66-67, 296.

7. Charles Y. Glock and Rodney Stark, *Christian Beliefs and Anti-Semitism* (New York, 1966).

8. Scoring: one point for each of the four statements with which the respondents agreed. Scores range from 0 to 4 with 0 ranking low, 1 or 2 moderate, and 3 or 4 high. Validation is assumed on the basis of face validity or logical validation.

9. Heinrich Bornkamm, *Luther's World of Thought,* trans. by Martin H. Bertram (St. Louis, 1965), p. 229.

10. Scoring: one point for each liberal answer, with scores ranging from 0 to 3. Scores of 0 or 1 were ranked low, 2 moderate, and 3 high. To test for validation we asked respondents to agree or disagree with the statement "There should be controls on science so that changes won't come too fast." Fifty-five percent ranking low, 35 percent moderate, and 20 percent high on the Civil Liberties Index agreed, thus attesting to validity of the index.

11. Samuel A. Stouffer, *Communism, Conformity, and Civil Liberties* (New York, 1966), pp. 142-55.

Chapter V

1. Weber, *The Protestant Ethic*, p. 85.

2. Scoring: one point was given for each answer in which strong or harsh treatment was recommended. Scores ranged from 0 to 3 with 0 ranking low, 1 moderate, and 2 or 3 high. For validation the laymen's answers to another question regarding the treatment of deviants were considered. An agree-disagree answer was requested for the statement "We should spend less time trying to find new ways to handle juvenile delinquency and return to the old methods of discipline." Fifty-three percent ranking low, 64 percent moderate, and 78 percent high on the Treatment of Deviance Index agreed, thus suggesting a high predictive capability for the index.

3. If individuals indicated more than one action (which was rare), only the first one mentioned is included in this tabulation.

4. Scores ranged from 0 to 3. A score of 0 or 1 was ranked low, 2 moderate, and 3 high. For validation see Table A-36.

5. If an individual indicated more than one action (which was rare), only the first one mentioned was included in this tabulation.

Chapter VI

1. See for example J. Howard Pew, "Should the Church 'Meddle' in Civil Affairs?," *Reader's Digest* (May 1966) and Hadden, *The Gathering Storm*.

2. These findings are similar to Lenski's, pp. 154-55.

3. See Hadden, pp. 164-79.

4. Scores on the Social Action Index range from 0 to 4. Zero and 1 were ranked low, 2 or 3 moderate, and 4 high. See Table A-44 for validation.

5. *The Lutheran Hymnal* (St. Louis, 1941). This hymnal is currently used by the Missouri and Wisconsin synods.

Chapter VII

1. One point was given for each answer which conformed with the traditional Lutheran doctrine of original sin. The scores range from 0 to 3. Those with scores of 0 or 1 were ranked low, 2 moderate, and 3 high. For validation see Table A-50.

2. One point was given for each answer stressing God's will. Range: 0 to 4, with a score of 0 or 1 low, 2 moderate, and 3 or 4 high. For validation see Table A-52.

3. See Talcott Parsons, "Religion in a Modern Pluralistic Society," *Review of Religious Research*, VII (Spring 1966), p. 141.

4. The exact wording is: "How do you think man is saved?" a) by action and works, b) by devotion, c) by knowledge, or d) by God's grace.

5. For complete data on these social variables, see the author's Ph.D. dissertation.

6. The percentages of laymen choosing to obey included 20 percent age 30 or under; 20 percent age 31-40; 23 percent age 41-50; 23 percent age 51-60; and 39 percent age 61 and over. For the clergy the percentages are none age 30 and under; 13 percent age 31-40; 32 percent age 41-50; 40 percent 51-60; and 65 percent age 61 and over.

7. Weber, *The Protestant Ethic* and Troeltsch, *The Social Teaching of the Christian Churches.*

8. Bernard Lazerwitz, "A Comparison of Major Religious Groups," *Journal of the American Statistical Association,* LVI (September 1961), p. 574.

9. Albert J. Mayer and Harry Sharp, "Religious Preference and Worldly Success," *American Sociological Review,* XXVII (April 1962), pp. 218-27.

10. Christen T. Jonassen, "The Protestant Ethic and the Spirit of Capitalism in Norway," *American Sociological Review,* XII (1947), pp. 676-86.

11. W. Seward Salisbury, *Religion in American Culture* (Homewood, Ill., 1964), pp. 345-46.

12. One point was given for each answer emphasizing salvation with scores ranging from 0 to 3. Scores of 0 or 1 were ranked low, a score of 2 was ranked moderate, and a score of 3 was ranked high. Logical validation or face validity was assumed.

13. One point was given for each answer stressing the importance of moral behavior, with total scores ranging from 0 to 3. Those with a score of 0 or 1 were ranked low, a score of 2 was ranked moderate, and a score of 3 was ranked high. Logical validation or face validity was assumed.

14. Exact percentages of laymen ranking high on the Moral Conduct Index by age are as follows: age 30 or under, 38 percent; age 31-40, 45 percent; age 41-50, 47 percent; age 51-60, 56 percent; and age 61 and over, 66 percent.

Chapter VIII

1. The analysis of the student data constitutes only one chapter, and space limits the discussion and interpretation of these findings. Consequently, considerable selectivity of questions and indexes to be analyzed and some limitation on depth of discussion is necessary. This chapter compares members from the following denominational groups with the total number of respondents from each group indicated in parentheses: Baptist (92); Episcopalian (41); Jewish (58); Lutheran—ALC (53); Lutheran—LCA (27); Lutheran—MS (70); Lutheran—WS (42); Presbyterian (92); Roman Catholic (305); United Church of Christ (34); United Methodist (143).

2. See Chapter Two for details on the construction of the various indexes of religious commitment.

3. For complete data the reader is referred to the author's dissertation.

4. Because of space limitations religious knowledge is not discussed. See

Table A-57 for rankings on this index. Note some of the questions involved the New Testament with which Jews would be less familiar.

5. A 1969 study at Eastern Michigan University showed that nearly 50 percent of the students had smoked marijuana.

6. Stark and Glock, *American Piety.*

7. Hadden, *The Gathering Storm.*

Chapter IX

1. For data from other studies supporting this trend, see Stark and Glock, *American Piety,* and Hadden, *The Gathering Storm.*

2. Stark and Glock, *American Piety,* p. 208.

3. Stark and Glock in *American Piety* first noted this trend in their church membership study in Northern California and their national sample of adult Americans.

4. George Gallup Poll, *The New York Times,* June 1, 1969.

5. Hadden, p. 207.

6. For a discussion on the self-fulfilling prophecy, see Robert K. Merton, *Social Theory and Social Structure* (Glencoe, Ill., 1949), pp. 129, 421-36.

7. For discussion of the problems involved in carrying out the comfort and challenge functions of religion among Episcopalians, see Glock, Ringer, and Babbie, *To Comfort and to Challenge.*

8. Hadden, p. 222.

9. Hadden's data in *The Gathering Storm* supports this conclusion.

10. Nine percent of the clergy ranking moderate on the Religious Beliefs Index say they have thought very seriously of leaving the ministry, and 18 percent say they have considered it. Of those who are most theologically conservative 9 percent have thought seriously of leaving the ministry and another 16 percent said they have considered it.

11. Talcott Parsons, *The Social System* (Glencoe, Ill., 1951), pp. 371-72.

12. Usually multiple questions were used to determine a clergyman's liberal or conservative stand on an issue. In a few cases as many as five questions determined an individual's position.

Appendix I
Methodology

THIS STUDY investigated the four largest branches of Lutheranism—the American Lutheran Church (ALC), the Lutheran Church in America (LCA), the Lutheran Church —Missouri Synod (MS), and the Wisconsin Evangelical Lutheran Synod (WS). These bodies comprise more than 98 percent of the Lutheran membership in the United States.* The geographical area of the study was most of the three-county area of metropolitan Detroit.

Three separate surveys were conducted—a random sample interview survey of Lutheran laymen within the study area, a mailed questionnaire sent to every Lutheran parish clergyman within the boundaries, and a mailed questionnaire sent to a random sample of college students attending Eastern Michigan University in Ypsilanti.

INTERVIEWS OF LUTHERAN LAYMEN

To make some quantitative evaluation of the impact of religious commitment on the total life orientation of individuals, and to determine whether or not the spirit of the Lutheran ethic continues to exist, a scientific random sample of Lutheran church members was interviewed. Although more expensive and time consuming, the advantages of a personal interview for this phase of the study far outweighted the value of a mailed questionnaire. The low rate of response from mailed questionnaires—usually ranging from 40 to 70 percent—allows the possibility of an unknown source of error which affects the reliability of the findings. Also, since religious knowledge was an important factor being investigated, the interview situation prevented the respondents from seeking help on these questions.

Sampling Procedure

A sample of Lutheran church members, which represented scientifically all laymen in each branch of Lutheranism within the study boundaries, was drawn. The simplest and least expensive method of taking such a sample was from local churches' confirmed or communicant membership lists. It should be noted that such lists are not always up-to-date, often contain inaccurate addresses, and on occasion, have been said to be "padded" with extra names. Regardless of these disadvantages, the membership lists were still the most accessible source for drawing the sample. The fact that these lists probably contained many marginal members was not considered to be a limitation, since the study sought to interview Lutherans who varied greatly in their degree of religious involvement and commitment. Individuals who were found to have changed to other, non-Lutheran religions were not interviewed.

Because of the particular topics considered, only those 21 years of age or over, or those under 21 who were cur-

---

*Baptized membership totals as of 1969 were 3,279,517 for the Lutheran Church in America; 2,870,355 for the Lutheran Church—Missouri Synod; 2,575,300 for the American Lutheran Church; and 371,048 for the Wisconsin Evangelical Lutheran Synod.

rently married, were interviewed. In practically all cases churches sent membership lists to our research office for the purpose of drawing the sample. Only a small number of churches refused to cooperate in the process. Three Wisconsin Synod churches refused to let their membership lists be used, two relatively small churches with 170 and 196 members, and a third quite large, with 727 members. One church was located in the city of Detroit and the two others in the suburbs. These nonparticipating churches showed no unique features when compared to the thirteen other Wisconsin Synod churches which did cooperate. Six Missouri Synod churches refused to participate in the process of drawing the sample. However, 115 Missouri Synod churches did participate. Four of the nonparticipating churches were located within the city of Detroit and the other two in suburban areas. There were no unique features about these six churches that would affect the overall validity of the study. The churches were well scattered geographically and varied widely in membership size. All churches from the Lutheran Church in America (59) and the American Lutheran Church (47) cooperated in the sample selection process by sending in their church membership lists.

Ten Missouri Synod churches and two Wisconsin Synod churches indicated that they had constitutional regulations preventing them from sending a list of church members. These churches, however, still agreed to help in the sample selection. In these cases, the local pastor or church secretary provided names and addresses from an alphabetical listing of lay membership. This relinquished some control over the sample selection, since it was necessary to trust local ministers and church secretaries to give the exact names according to specified random numbers and make no substitutions. There may have been some temptation on the part of individual clergymen to pick their "better" or "more religious" members to be interviewed. Two groups of names received appeared highly suspicious, but they were still utilized as part of the total sample. On the whole, however, the random samples seemed representative of the membership in each of the four Lutheran groups within the study boundaries. The total number of churches in the four Lutheran bodies within the study boundary area, and the number of churches cooperating in the sample drawing process, are indicated in the following table.

Branch	Number of Churches	Number of Churches in Sample	Percentage of Churches Represented in Sample
ALC	47	47	100
LCA	59	59	100
MS	121	115	95
WS	16	13	81
Total	243	234	96

Some local clergymen were apprehensive about having their members interviewed, perhaps because they feared their members' responses to certain questions which would reflect on their ministry and teaching. Each clergyman was assured that no comparisons would be made by or between local congregations. Despite this assurance, however, a few clergymen continued to feel uneasy about the study.

A primary objective was to have approximately an equal number of respondents from each of the four branches of Lutheranism in the total sample. Since the total number of of members from each of the four groups living in the Detroit area varied greatly, names were selected using different interval numbers for each branch of Lutheranism. A random number was used to draw the first respondent, from the first church, in an alphabetical listing of churches. After the initial name was drawn, every *Nth* name thereafter was chosen. The above table shows the number of respondents drawn in the original sample from each Lutheran body.

Of the 1,296 names drawn in the original sample, 266 were excluded for being under age 21 (or not married), deceased, presently in the armed forces, away at college, no longer a Lutheran church member, or no longer living in the study area. The completion rate for the total sample was 86 percent and the refusal rate was only 12 percent.

Branch	Number of Congregations Participating	Total Number of Members in the Participating Congregations	Interval Number (N)	Original Number of Respondents in Sample
ALC	47	30,485	100	304
LCA	59	20,880	60	348
MS	115	78,100	250	312
WS	13	3,323	10	332

The interview schedule was developed over nine months, during which extensive pretests and critical evaluations were made. Questions were submitted to clergymen, theologians, and sociologists for criticism. Many questions from previous studies in sociology of religion were used, particularly from the research of Charles Glock, Gerhard Lenski, and Jeffrey Hadden.

A total of 213 questions were included in the final draft of the interview schedule. Almost all were of the structured type, with a choice of specific answers provided. Only about

ten questions were the open-ended type. The most common
form of question offered a four-point continuum of agree-
disagree answers, ranging from: 1) agree; 2) probably agree

	ALC	LCA	MS	WS	TOTAL
Total number in original sample	304	348	312	332	1,296
Excluded from sample Under 21 (or not married if under 21)	59	45	32	54	190
Deceased	1	2	2	4	9
In armed forces	2	0	3	3	8
Away at college	3	3	0	3	9
No longer Lutheran	0	3	1	1	5
Moved out of study area or could not be located	10	16	9	10	45
Total	75	69	47	75	266
Number to be interviewed	229	279	265	257	1,030
Noninterviews resulting from ill- ness, incapacitation, language or communication problems	3	5	11	4	23
Respondents switching to an- other branch of Lutheranism	−2	−1	+3	0	—
Refusals	32	31	34	24	121
Number of completed interviews	192	242	223	229	886
Completion rate *(By Percentage)*	85	87	83	89	86
Refusal rate (By Percentage)	14	11	13	9	12

or agree somewhat; 3) probably disagree or disagree somewhat; and 4) disagree. To simplify the analysis throughout

the book, unless otherwise indicated all agree-type responses are grouped together and all disagree-type responses are grouped together.

Respondents were allowed to answer "don't know" to questions they felt they could not answer. Through this means the clergymen, particularly, were asked to criticize any question they thought was poorly worded. The few questions receiving a significant number of "don't know" responses or other critical comments were omitted. Such a procedure of criticism and elimination insured additional validity for each question.

The average time for an interview was slightly less than ninety minutes, with many completed within one hour. A few lasted as long as three hours. Although the interview was a relatively long one by survey research standards, only one session was cut off for this reason and most of the respondents indicated that they enjoyed expressing their opinions.

Many interviewers were recruited from local Lutheran congregations, and only those with recommended interviewing qualifications were used. Most had some college education, previous interviewing experience, or recommendations from their ministers as being well suited for this work. Lutheran parochial school teachers and clergymen, as well as many sociology students from Wayne State University, also served as interviewers. One professional interviewer, employed full-time on the study for almost one year, concentrated primarily on first refusals and callbacks. Approximately 75 people worked as interviewers. All were trained, were provided with a handbook of interviewing instructions, and were required to carry out practice interviews. The high completion rate of 86 percent is reflective of the time and effort exerted to make the interviewing phase of the study scientifically sound.

Prior to the interview laymen received a letter explaining the nature of the study. The initial letter indicated that the study was being conducted through Wayne State Univer-

Branch	Number of Clergy in Sample	Number of Questionnaires Returned	Percentage of Questionnaires Returned
ALC	56	54	96
LCA	57	54	95
MS			
Michigan District	116	94	81
English District	25	23	92
MS (districts combined)	141	117	83
WS	16	16	100
Total	270	241	89

sity. Followup letters were sent to all persons whom the interviewers were unable to contact. (See pp. 242-45)

SURVEY OF LUTHERAN CLERGYMEN

The attitudes, values, and behavioral patterns of Lutheran clergymen were also surveyed. In this case, an anonymous questionnaire seemed to provide the best possible means of getting honest answers. Each Lutheran parish clergyman within the study area received a copy of the questionnaire, with the majority of questions the same as those asked of laymen. A few questions from the lay interview schedules were excluded, such as the items on religious knowledge, religious practices, and associational involvement. Additional questions asked of the clergymen related to theological controversies, challenges facing the church, social action, seminary training, traditional church programs, and ecumenical activities.

SURVEY OF COLLEGE STUDENTS

The third population surveyed was college students, a random sample of the entire student body at one university. The sample afforded the opportunity to compare the attitudes, values, and behavior of Lutheran students with those of other faiths. The sample is only representative of students at one university and does not represent all young people of college age, or all college students.

The sample was drawn from Eastern Michigan University, a state university in the metropolitan Detroit area located approximately thirty miles from the center of Detroit. At the time that the sample was drawn, the enrollment was approximately 15,000 students, including 3,500 graduate students. Only a few came from out-of-state, and approximately 80 percent came from within a forty-mile radius of Detroit.

The student sample was drawn from the official *1968 Directory—Eastern Michigan University*. Compilers of this directory informed us that the information on students' addresses was possibly only 75 per cent correct, because the information had been collected in August, one month before school officially began. Many students had not yet made campus housing arrangements, and others made changes when they arrived. Attempts were made to further check names and addresses drawn in the sample with up-to-date University residence hall lists, University housing division records, telephone company listings, and campus police. Late registrants, many of them graduate students, were not included in the directory and thus were not part of the sample.

DETROIT METROPOLITAN LUTHERAN RESEARCH AND PLANNING STUDY

lawrence kersten, director · 17129 bosworth court · detroit, michigan 48219 · telephone 313-538-1662 · 533-2006

May 26, 1967

We are now in the last phase of our study of Lutheranism here in the Detroit area. The final segment of our data gathering process involves a study of Lutheran clergy.

Enclosed you will find a questionnaire dealing primarily with your attitudes, values, and feelings about religion and the Lutheran Church. We would appreciate your completing the questionnaire as soon as possible and returning it in the enclosed pre-stamped envelope.

Although the questionnaire appears long, most of the answers will be short and you should be able to finish the entire questionnaire in one hour. All questionnaires are completely confidential. There are no identification numbers on the forms and we are asking you to please not sign your name.

It is my sincere hope that you will enjoy answering these questions and use this opportunity to express your true feelings. If you have any questions or comments, please feel free to call me at my office or home (538-1662 or 464-9929). Many thanks for your help and cooperation.

Sincerely,

Lawrence K. Kersten
Research Director

epk
Enclosures

GENERAL COMMITTEE: *charles sandrock, chairman · robert robinson, secretary · donald lawrence, treasurer · karl boehmke
james cross · harold hecht · paul heinecke · george fleischer · ronald fuller · richard jackson · walter kloetzli,
advisory member · clarence larson · reuben schmidt · e.c. weber · e.a. westcott · robert wietelmann · martin vents*

The Lutheran Ethic

DETROIT METROPOLITAN LUTHERAN RESEARCH AND PLANNING STUDY

lawrence kersten, director · 17129 bosworth court · detroit, michigan 48219 · telephone 313-538-1662 · 533-2006

Since we have had a number of clergymen tell us that they have
lost or misplaced their questionnaire, I thought I would write
to you to see if this may have happened in your case. If this
is your situation, please mail back to us the enclosed post card
indicating that you want us to send you another copy of the questionnaire.

As of this date we have by far the majority of the questionnaires
returned. From the coments that came in along with the questionnaires, it appears that most respondents found it an interesting
experience. We are still very much interested in your viewpoints
and hope you can complete your questionnaire soon.

If our records are incorrect and you have already completed and
mailed back your questionnaire, possibly we never received the
post card you were to mail back at the same time. Please call
our office to correct this situation, if this is the case.
(Phone 538-1662).

If you have any questions about the study, please feel free to
call or write me at anytime. I hope you will be able to find one
hour yet this month to complete and return the questionnaire to
us.

Many thanks for your help and cooperation.

                                        Sincerely,

                                        Lawrence K. Kersten
                                        Research Director

LKK/ek

Appendix I

 WAYNE STATE UNIVERSITY

DETROIT, MICHIGAN 48202

Wayne State University is currently conducting a study
of religion in American life. You have been selected to
be interviewed on the basis of a scientific random sample
of church members living in the Detroit area. Your name
was drawn from church lists and for the sake of scientific
accuracy it is important that there be no substitutes.

Your Pastor, who has been consulted about this study,
feels, as I hope you will, that it will produce a useful
picture of American religion and will also be extremely
valuable for local church planning. You will simply be
asked to give your opinions and attitudes on a series of
questions dealing with the topic of religion. There will
be no right or wrong answers. We simply want to find out
how you feel about certain issues.

All answers and statements are strictly confidential.
Names or other identification are never used on the questionnaire and no person or address is ever identified.
Even your Pastor does not and will not know who is interviewed from his church. Only summaries of statements will
be published--such as "Three persons out of ten reported
that. . ."

One of our interviewers will be calling on you in the next
week or so and we are confident that you will find this
a most interesting study in which to participate. Your
generosity in giving your time and effort to assist in this
study is very deeply appreciated.

                         Sincerely,

                         Lawrence K. Kersten

LKK/epk

The Lutheran Ethic

 WAYNE STATE UNIVERSITY

DETROIT, MICHIGAN 48202

Several weeks ago I sent you a letter asking for your cooperation
in connection with a study of religion here in the Detroit area.
I am writing to you again at this time because our records indicate
our contact with you was never completed. I realize that my first
letter did not make clear the purposes of this study and I hope
that this letter will overcome this problem.

The four Lutheran denominations in the Detroit area (American
Lutheran Church, Lutheran Church in America, Lutheran Church--
Missouri Synod, and Lutheran Church--Wisconsin Synod) are the
sponsors of this study. The Lutheran Church leaders from these
denominations are trying to obtain objective and confidential
opinions from church members on how they view the Lutheran Church.
We want to obtain the attitudes of both active and inactive members.

Let me emphasize that we are simply interested in your opinions
and views on the job that the church is doing or not doing. It
should be stressed that all interviews remain confidential and not
even your pastor knows who is and who is not being interviewed
from his church. Your pastor does express the hope however, that
all of those chosen in the sample will give about an hour of their
time for the interview.

Remember you were chosen purely by chance and to ensure scientific
accuracy no substitutions can be made. In light of the help that
this study will be to the churches generally, and to your denomination in particular, I hope that you will find it possible to
cooperate with us.

Please feel free to call me at our field office (538-1662 or
538-1218) if you have further questions or comments about the study.

Sincerely,

Lawrence K. Kersten
Research Director

LKK/epk

In drawing the student sample a rough estimate of the number of students of each religious faith was obtained from religious preference cards filled out during registration. It

Number in original sample	1,498
No longer in school, or could not locate	201
Nonrespondents	312
Complete questionnaires	985
Percentage returning questionnaires	76*

*Percentage excludes students who could not be located.

was decided that an 11 percent sample of the entire student body would be necessary to have sufficient numbers for statistical analysis in each major denominational group. An estimated 13,600 names of students were included in the alphabetical listing in the directory. A random number between 1 and 9 was drawn to determine the first person in the sample, and every 9th name thereafter was chosen, yielding a total sample of 1,498. Several of these names included no addresses or were listed with incorrect addresses. Many students could not be found and possibly never finally enrolled. A complete breakdown of the random sample of the student population, as well as the overall return rate on the questionnaires, is indicated.

As a measure of the representativeness of the student sample, the sample was compared to the actual percentages of students in each class level. The following table shows the percentages of sample students at different class levels as compared with the actual percentages in each class. These results show that the random sample of students is thus quite representative of the student body. The underrepresentation of graduate students was expected. The slightly larger percentages of upperclassmen (juniors and seniors) compensates somewhat for this problem.

	Percentages in Sample*	Actual Percentages in University
Freshmen	27	27
Sophomores	20	21
Juniors	20	16
Seniors	18	13
Graduate Students	15	23

*These figures do not include additional Lutheran subsample.

In addition to the random sample of all students, an independent subsample of Lutheran students was drawn. This subsample increased the number of questionnaires filled out by Lutheran students, so that valid statistical comparisons could be made among the students identifying with the various branches of Lutheranism and the students identifying with other major denominations.

University campus chaplains provided lists of Lutheran students, and separate lists were available for Missouri Synod and Wisconsin Synod students. Since the American Lutheran Church and the Lutheran Church in America cooperate on student campus work, a combined list of ALC and LCA students was available, but this list did not differentiate between ALC and LCA student affiliation.

Additional Lutheran students were, of course, drawn in the random sample of the entire student population. The number of Lutheran students to be drawn in the additional subsample was determined after an estimate was made of the proportion of students in each branch of Lutheranism in the entire Lutheran student population. The number of names drawn in the Lutheran subsample for each branch of Lutheranism is shown in a table.

Branch	Total Names on List	Interval Number	Total Names Drawn
MS	339	17	22
WS	53	every name	53
ALC	115*	3	39
LCA	115*	3	39
Total for Additional Lutheran Subsample:			153

*Estimated.

Return rates for the Lutheran subsample are as indicated in a table.

Number of names originally drawn in Lutheran subsample (excluding duplicate names from random sample of whole student population—16)	137
Total no longer in school, or could not be located	8
Total nonrespondents	19
Total questionnaires returned	110
Percentage questionnaires returned	85*

*Excludes students who could not be located.

VALIDATION OF INDEXES

An index is considered to possess validity when it actually measures what it claims to measure. (For a discussion of the

Belief Statements	Sample	Low	Moderate	High
It is possible for someone to reject the virgin birth of Christ and still be a good Christian. (Disagree)*	Lay	29	68	80
	Clergy	2	45	83
I believe in the devil as an active and evil being in the world. (Agree)*	Lay	47	73	88
	Clergy	27	88	99
A Lutheran can accept a view of the evolution of man from lower forms of animals as quite possible. (Disagree)*	Lay	31	56	80
	Clergy	6	41	87
It is not as important to worry about life after death as about what one can do in this life. (Disagree)*	Lay	13	36	56
	Clergy	9	25	69

$p = .001$ in all cases

*Theologically most conservative response.

Note: All other validation tables for indexes are found in Appendix II.

concept of validity, see Goode and Hart, *Methods of Social Research*.) The tests used in connection with the Religious Beliefs Index provide an illustration of the process involved in determining validity.

In addition to logical validation or face validity, two other techniques were employed to verify that a high degree of confidence can be placed in the Religious Beliefs Index. One technique for determining validity is the so-called "known group" method. A "known group," in terms of theological conservatism, is the Wisconsin Synod, which is proud to be known as a theologically very conservative Lutheran body. If the Religious Beliefs Index is measuring theological beliefs validly, then the conservatism of the "known group" should be reflected in the data. Furthermore, if any subgroup of a religious body should truly reflect its belief system and theological stance, it should be the clergy. Thus, it would be expected that most of the Wisconsin Synod clergy would rank high or most conservative on the Religious Beliefs Index. This is exactly what occurred. Every Wisconsin Synod clergyman gave the most conservative answer to each of the four questions in the index. This 100 percent consensus greatly attests to the validity of the Religious Beliefs Index.

Another measure of validity involves the prediction capabilities of the index in question. If an index can be used to predict the answers to other related questions, this can be taken as evidence of its validity. The respondents' answers to four other belief questions were compared with their rankings on the Religious Beliefs Index (see Belief Statements table). On the basis of an individual's ranking on the index, his responses to other questions can be predicted with a high degree of accuracy.

Appendix II

ADDITIONAL TABLES

TABLE A-1
Clergy Rankings on the Religious Beliefs Index, By Age

Age	(N)	Low	By Percentage Moderate	High
30 and under	(31)	55	29	16
31 — 40	(84)	39	30	31
41 — 50	(57)	19	21	60
51 — 60	(36)	14	44	42
61 and over	(20)	0	25	75

$p = .001$

TABLE A-2
Lay Rankings on the Religious Beliefs Index, By Social Class

Social Class	(N)	Low	By Percentage Moderate	High
Lower	(251)	20	46	34
Middle	(459)	26	42	32
Upper	(123)	35	35	30

$p = .05$

TABLE A-3
*Lay Rankings on the Religious Beliefs Index,
By Type of Community in Which Reared*

Place of Rearing	(N)	Low	By Percentage Moderate	High
In a large city	(400)	29	43	28
In a medium-sized city	(120)	29	42	29
In a small town	(205)	25	39	36
On a farm	(146)	13	45	42

$p = .05$

TABLE A-4
*Lay Rankings on the Religious Beliefs Index,
By How Respondent Became a Member of the Lutheran Church*

How Respondent Became a Member	(N)	Low	By Percentage Moderate	High
Family, influence as a child	(545)	22	41	37
Renewed (previously family)	(33)	36	40	24
Through marriage	(129)	36	35	29
Conversion from another religious faith (not at marriage)	(145)	24	55	21
Conversion from no religious faith (not at marriage)	(26)	15	54	31

$p = .001$

TABLE A-5
Lay Rankings on the Associational Involvement Index, By Social Class

Social Class	Low	By Percentage Moderate	High
Lower	36	36	28
Middle	33	30	37
Upper	27	27	46

$p = .05$

TABLE A-6
Lay Rankings on the Associational Involvement Index,
By How Respondent Became a Member of the Lutheran Church

How Respondent Became a Member	(N)	Low	By Percentage Moderate	High
Family, influence as a child	(546)	32	31	37
Renewed (previously family)	(32)	38	43	19
Through marriage	(130)	40	32	28
Conversion from another faith (not a marriage)	(145)	27	36	37
Conversion from no religious faith (not a marriage)	(27)	33	19	48

$p = $ NS

TABLE A-7
Lay Rankings on the Associational Involvement Index, By Age

Age	Low	By Percentage Moderate	High
30 and under	41	31	28
31 — 40	33	32	35
41 — 50	33	26	41
51 — 60	32	33	35
61 and over	27	40	33

$p = $ NS

TABLE A-8
Validation of the Religious Practices Index

		Ranking on Index, By Percentage			
	Answer	Low	Moderate	High
About how often do you pray; that is, alone as an individual and not as part of a group or congregation?	Several times a day	4	16	44
	Once a week or less	36	18	4
How often do you ask forgiveness for your sins?	Very often	20	36	63
	Occasionally or never	40	24	10
How often do you read any religious newspapers or magazines received in your home?	Every issue	29	41	59
	Almost never	14	7	1
How often do you read any of the devotional booklets distributed by your denomination?	Daily	11	14	31
	Just every now and then	51	43	28
Do you ever make a point of listening to or watching religious services on radio or television?	Yes, regularly	7	14	22
	No, never or practically never	43	30	15
How often do you have occasion to read the Bible?	Very often	3	6	29
	Never	15	5	1

$p = .001$ for all questions

TABLE A-9
Lay Rankings on the Religious Practices Index, By Place of Rearing

Place of Rearing	Low	By Percentage Moderate	High
Large city	38	28	34
Medium-sized city	21	38	31
Small town	32	33	35
Farm	25	32	43

$p = $ NS

TABLE A-10
Lay Rankings on the Religious Practices Index,
By How Respondent Became a Member of the Lutheran Church

How Respondent Became Lutheran	Low	By Percentage Moderate	High
Family influence as a child	31	32	37
Renewed (previously family)	40	39	21
Through marriage	41	33	26
Conversion from another faith (not at marriage)	32	30	38
Conversion from no religious faith (not at marriage)	23	35	42

$p = $ NS

TABLE A-11
Lay Rankings on the Religious Knowledge Index, By Social Class

Social Class	Low	By Percentage Moderate	High
Lower	33	40	27
Middle	23	36	41
Upper	9	48	43

$p = .001$

TABLE A-12
Lay Rankings on the Religious Knowledge Index, By Nationality

Nationality	(*N*)	Low	By Percentage Moderate	High
German	(385)	22	33	45
Scandinavian	(219)	29	43	28

$p = .01$

TABLE A-13
Lay Rankings on the Religious Knowledge Index,
By How Respondent Became a Lutheran

	Low	By Percentage Moderate	High
Family influence as a child	25	35	40
Renewed (previously family)	27	52	21
Through marriage	26	44	30
Conversion from another religious faith (not at marriage)	21	44	35
Conversion from no religious faith (not at marriage)	30	40	30

TABLE A-14

Validation of the Communal Involvement Index

	Ranking on Index, By Percentage		
	Low	Moderate	High
Most friends they associate with outside of church affairs are Lutheran	12	20	35
Three or four of their four closest friends are Lutherans	18	35	49
Most of their relatives on their side of the family are Lutheran	44	61	75
Have never belonged to another denomination other than Lutheran	54	70	84
Their denomination should provide Lutheran parochial elementary and high schools	65	69	83
Became a member of the Lutheran Church through their family, as a child.	47	66	79

$p = .001$ for all questions

TABLE A-15

Lay Rankings on Communal Involvement Index, By Social Class

	By Percentage		
Social Class	Low	Moderate	High
Lower	36	43	21
Middle	34	51	15
Upper	29	58	13

$p = .05$

TABLE A-16

Lay Rankings on the Communal Involvement Index,
By Type of Community in Which Reared

Community		By Percentage	
	Low	Moderate	High
Large city	37	48	15
Medium-sized city	33	53	14
Small town	33	51	16
Farm	23	51	26

$p = .05$

TABLE A-17

Lay Rankings on the Communal Involvement Index,
By How Respondent Became a Lutheran

	Rankings, By Percentage		
	Low	Moderate	High
Family influence as a child	24	54	22
Renewed (previously family)	42	46	12
Through marriage	45	47	8
Conversion from another religious faith (not at marriage)	51	41	8
Conversion from no religious faith (not at marriage)	31	50	19

$p = .001$

TABLE A-18

Clergy Identification with the Republican Party,
By Rankings on the Religious Beliefs Index, Controlled for Age

Age	Ranking	Percentage Republican or Closer to Republican Party
30 and under	Low	24 (25)
	Moderate	64 (11)
	High	97 (6)
31 — 40	Low	31 (49)
	Moderate	54 (35)
	High	66 (32)
41 — 50	Low	57 (14)
	Moderate	71 (14)
	High	69 (39)
51 — 60	Low	43 (7)
	Moderate	61 (18)
	High	74 (19)
61 and over	Low	* (0)
	Moderate	* (5)
	High	50 (22)

*Number of cases too small to compute statistically reliable percentages.

TABLE A-19

Lay Identification with the Republican Party,
By Rankings on the Communal Involvement Index,
Controlled for Social Class

Social Class	Rankings	Percentage Republican or Closer to Republican Party
Lower	Low	30 (118)
	Moderate	33 (141)
	High	49 (59)
Middle	Low	30 (210)
	Moderate	41 (313)
	High	52 (87)
Upper	Low	53 (43)
	Moderate	62 (89)
	High	62 (21)

TABLE A-20

Validation of the Social Welfare Index (Lay Data)

	Ranking by Percentage		
	Low	Moderate	High
Most people who live in poverty could do something about their situation if they really wanted to. (Agreeing) $p = .001$	67	54	31
Many jobs go unfilled because a lot of people would rather live off welfare than work. (Agreeing) $p = .001$	66	60	30
If you give a lot of help to people who are having a hard time, many of them will begin thinking they have it coming to them. (Agreeing) $p = .001$	66	**57**	**39**
Our country would be better off if people would go along with the idea that "God helps those who help themselves." (Agreeing) $p = .001$	35	27	9
Respondents preferring Goldwater in 1964 Presidential election	48	28	23

TABLE A-21

Clergy and Lay Rankings on the Social Welfare Index, By Type and Degree of Religious Commitment

			By Percentage		
Sample	Index	Ranking	Low	Moderate	High
Clergy	Beliefs $(p = .001)$	Low	11	23	66
		Moderate	29	29	42
		High	51	26	23
Lay	Beliefs $(p = NS)$	Low	33	30	37
		Moderate	30	30	40
		High	37	27	36
Lay	Associational Involvement $(p = NS)$	Low	33	28	39
		Moderate	35	25	40
		High	31	34	35
Lay	Communal Involvement $(p = NS)$	Low	29	29	42
		Moderate	35	30	35
		High	33	30	37
Lay	Practices $(p = NS)$	Low	34	31	35
		Moderate	34	29	37
		High	32	28	40
Lay	Knowledge $(p = .001)$	Low	20	26	54
		Moderate	36	30	34
		High	38	31	31

TABLE A-22

Lay and Clergy Attitudes on War,
By Type and Degree of Religious Commitment

Sample	Index	Ranking	Send troops to Cuba before Castro became so powerful. (Agreeing)	Bomb North Vietnam with everything we have. (Agreeing)
Clergy	Beliefs	Low	20	9
		Moderate	26	15
		High	38	38
		($p = .01$)	($p = .001$)
Lay	Beliefs	Low	41	35
		Moderate	49	39
		High	45	39
		($p = $ NS)	($p = $ NS)
Lay	Associational Involvement	Low	46	42
		Moderate	43	36
		High	47	35
		($p = $ NS)	($p = $ NS)
Lay	Communal Involvement	Low	42	40
		Moderate	46	36
		High	51	39
		($p = .05$)	($p = $ NS)
Lay	Practices	Low	44	37
		Moderate	46	40
		High	47	36
		($p = $ NS)	($p = $ NS)
Lay	Knowledge	Low	54	39
		Moderate	46	37
		High	39	38
		($p = .01$)	($p = $ NS)

TABLE A-23

Validity Questions for Race Prejudice Index (Laymen)

	By Percentage		
	Low	Moderate	High
While men are spiritually equal in God's eyes, there are in fact basic differences in intelligence among the races. (Agreeing) $p = .001$	32	64	87
The separation of men into classes and groups is the direct result of God's will and should not be tampered with. (Agreeing) $p = .001$	11	19	59
A Lutheran minister should *not* agree to perform the marriage of a Negro and a white person. (Agreeing) $p = .001$	30	42	72
Civil rights would *not* be an acceptable topic for their minister to preach upon from the pulpit. (Agreeing) $p = .001$	18	34	50

TABLE A-24

Clergy and Lay Attitudes Toward Catholics,
By Type and Degree of Religious Commitment

Sample	Index	Ranking	By Percentage Catholics less fair in business dealings. (Agreeing)	Catholics trying to get too much power. (Yes)
Clergy	Beliefs	Low	2	14
		Moderate	4	26
		High	10	60
			(p = NS)	(p = .001)
Lay	Beliefs	Low	8	28
		Moderate	11	32
		High	10	31
			(p = NS)	(p = NS)
Lay	Associational Involvement	Low	12	32
		Moderate	10	30
		High	8	31
			(p = NS)	(p = NS)
Lay	Communal Involvement	Low	6	22
		Moderate	10	33
		High	18	39
			(p = .01)	(p = .001)
Lay	Practices	Low	8	28
		Moderate	9	29
		High	12	36
			(p = NS)	(p = NS)
Lay	Knowledge	Low	12	33
		Moderate	9	31
		High	9	29
			(p = NS)	(p = NS)

TABLE A-25

*Lay and Clergy Attitudes Toward Nonbelievers,
By Type and Degree of Religious Commitment*

Sample	Index	Ranking	A person who says there is no God is likely to hold dangerous political ideas. (Agreeing, by percentage)
Clergy	Beliefs ($p = .001$)	Low	6
		Moderate	29
		High	57
Lay	Beliefs ($p = .001$)	Low	48
		Moderate	69
		High	74
Lay	Associational Involvement ($p = $ NS)	Low	61
		Moderate	68
		High	67
Lay	Communal Involvement ($p = .001$)	Low	59
		Moderate	65
		High	78
Lay	Practices ($p = .001$)	Low	60
		Moderate	66
		High	70
Lay	Knowledge ($p = $ NS)	Low	69
		Moderate	65
		High	62

TABLE A-26

Lay and Clergy Attitudes on the State of Morals in American Society,
By Branch of Lutheranism

		By Percentage			
	Sample	LCA	ALC	MS	WS
They are pretty bad and getting worse.	Lay	57	64	69	68
	Clergy	47	53	80	86
They are pretty bad but not getting worse.	Lay	18	13	13	14
	Clergy	27	30	12	7
They are all right as they are and not getting worse.	Lay	6	9	2	5
	Clergy	6	2	2	0
They are pretty good but getting worse.	Lay	17	12	14	11
	Clergy	12	11	6	7
They are pretty good and getting better.	Lay	2	2	1	1
	Clergy	4	0	0	0
Don't know.	Lay	0	0	1	0
	Clergy	4	4	0	0

Lay — p = NS
Clergy — p = .001

Appendix II

TABLE A-27

Clergy and Lay Attitudes Toward Dancing, By Type and Degree of Religious Commitment

Sample	Index	Ranking	By Percentage Dancing is "not wrong"
Clergy	Beliefs ($p = .001$)	Low Moderate High	97 77 42
Lay	Beliefs ($p = .05$)	Low Moderate High	97 91 89
Lay	Associational Involvement ($p = $ NS)	Low Moderate High	94 94 89
Lay	Communal Involvement ($p = $ NS)	Low Moderate High	94 92 89
Lay	Practices ($p = .05$)	Low Moderate High	97 93 87
Lay	Knowledge ($p = $ NS)	Low Moderate High	94 94 90

TABLE A-28

Clergy and Lay Attitudes on Divorce,
By Type and Degree of Religious Commitment

| | | | By Percentage | |
Sample	Index	Ranking	Although never totally satisfactory, divorce is often the best solution. (No)	Lutheran ministers should not perform marriage of a divorced person. (No)
Clergy	Beliefs	Low	26	0
		Moderate	25	5
		High	54	3
			($p = .001$)	($p = $ NS)
Lay	Beliefs	Low	25	8
		Moderate	43	12
		High	46	16
			($p = .001$)	($p = .05$)
Lay	Associational Involvement	Low	37	9
		Moderate	39	15
		High	41	12
			($p = $ NS)	($p = $ NS)
Lay	Communal Involvement	Low	38	9
		Moderate	37	11
		High	49	22
			($p = .05$)	($p = .01$)
Lay	Practices	Low	33	11
		Moderate	42	11
		High	42	15
			($p = $ NS)	($p = $ NS)
Lay	Knowledge	Low	37	10
		Moderate	40	13
		High	40	13
			($p = $ NS)	($p = $ NS)

TABLE A-29

*Clergy and Lay Attitudes on the Secular Role of Women,
By Type and Degree of Religious Commitment*

Sample	Index	Ranking	By Percentage Roles of wife-mother and career woman are basically incompatible. (Agreeing)	Wife should have as much to say as husband in family decisions. (Disagreeing)
Clergy	Beliefs	Low	12	17
		Moderate	32	16
		High	41	43
			($p = .001$)	($p = .001$)
Lay	Beliefs	Low	38	4
		Moderate	44	10
		High	47	17
			($p = .05$)	($p = .01$)
Lay	Associational Involvement	Low	42	8
		Moderate	45	13
		High	43	10
			($p = $ NS)	($p = $ NS)
Lay	Communal Involvement	Low	38	8
		Moderate	45	10
		High	49	16
			($p = .05$)	($p = .05$)
Lay	Practices	Low	37	6
		Moderate	47	11
		High	45	14
			($p = $ NS)	($p = .05$)
Lay	Knowledge	Low	47	3
		Moderate	41	9
		High	41	17
			($p = $ NS)	($p = .01$)

TABLE A-30

Clergy and Lay Attitudes on Capital Punishment, Sex Criminals, and Homosexuals,
By Type and Degree of Religious Commitment

Sample	Index	Ranking	Murderers should get death penalty. (Agreeing)	By Percentage Sex criminals should be publicly whipped. (Agreeing)	Homosexuals should be put in prison. (Agreeing)
Clergy	Beliefs	Low	21	0	2
		Moderate	54	6	19
		High	89	15	30
			$(p = .001)$	$(p = .01)$	$(p = .001)$
Lay	Beliefs	Low	47	35	26
		Moderate	44	38	32
		High	49	38	36
			$(p = NS)$	$(p = NS)$	$(p = .05)$
Lay	Associational Involvement	Low	52	37	33
		Moderate	46	39	31
		High	43	35	32
			$(p = .05)$	$(p = NS)$	$(p = NS)$
Lay	Communal Involvement	Low	48	39	33
		Moderate	44	36	26
		High	55	41	46
			$(p = NS)$	$(p = NS)$	$(p = .001)$
Lay	Practices	Low	48	36	25
		Moderate	50	41	35
		High	43	36	46
			$(p = NS)$	$(p = NS)$	$(p = .05)$
Lay	Knowledge	Low	62	48	50
		Moderate	46	38	30
		High	38	30	23
			$(p = .001)$	$(p = .001)$	$(p = .001)$

TABLE A-31

*Clergy and Lay Rankings on the Treatment of Deviance Index,
By Type and Degree of Religious Commitment*

Sample	Index	Ranking	By Percentage		
			Low	Moderate	High
Clergy	Beliefs ($p = .001$)	Low	79	20	1
		Moderate	43	43	14
		High	11	53	36
Lay	Beliefs ($p = $ NS)	Low	36	32	32
		Moderate	33	33	34
		High	28	34	38
Lay	Associational Involvement ($p = $ NS)	Low	30	34	36
		Moderate	32	33	35
		High	34	33	33
Lay	Communal Involvement ($p = .05$)	Low	30	33	37
		Moderate	36	34	30
		High	22	32	46
Lay	Practices ($p = $ NS)	Low	31	39	30
		Moderate	30	30	40
		High	34	31	35
Lay	Knowledge ($p = .001$)	Low	19	28	53
		Moderate	30	36	34
		High	42	35	23

The Lutheran Ethic

TABLE A-32

*Clergy and Lay Attitudes on Violence and Sex in Movies and on TV,
By Type and Degree of Religious Commitment*

Sample	Index	Ranking	By Percentage Disturbed by violence and sex in movies and on TV? (Yes)
Clergy	Beliefs (p = NS)	Low	79
		Moderate	77
		High	90
Lay	Beliefs (p = .05)	Low	79
		Moderate	85
		High	89
Lay	Associational Involvement (p = .01)	Low	76
		Moderate	87
		High	91
Lay	Communal Involvement (p = .01)	Low	80
		Moderate	85
		High	93
Lay	Practices (p = .01)	Low	78
		Moderate	86
		High	91
Lay	Knowledge (p = NS)	Low	83
		Moderate	84
		High	87

TABLE A-33
Lay and Clergy Actions Against Violence and Sex in Movies and on Television, By Branch of Lutheranism

By Percentage

Type of Action Taken	Lay				Clergy			
	LCA	ALC	MS	WS	LCA	ALC	MS	WS
(N)	(44)	(38)	(44)	(37)	(21)	(27)	(70)	(10)
Indirect Action								
Discussed or talked about it with someone or a group	23	25	17	17	10	22	16	10
Took a poll	0	3	0	0	0	0	0	0
Avoidance items ("turn off TV," "don't attend movies," "selective viewing," "protect children from such things")	59	47	52	65	14	15	14	0
Publish notices of good movies	0	0	0	0	0	4	0	0
Prayer	0	5	2	0	0	0	0	10
Preached about it	0	0	0	0	29	7	23	60
Worked on review committee	0	0	0	0	0	0	1	10
Lecture or teach against it	0	0	0	0	10	11	16	10
Totals	82	82	72	84	62	59	70	100

Direct Individual Action

Vote for individuals who say they are against these things	5	0	5	5	0	0	0	0
Wrote letters (as an individual) to Hollywood, congressmen, producers, advertisers, stations, etc.	11	16	9	3	19	26	21	0
Signed petitions or complaints	2	0	2	0	0	0	0	0
Totals	18	16	16	8	19	26	21	0

Direct Group Action

Worked with or belonged to a group trying to do something about situation	0	0	5	5	19	15	9	0
Wrote letters as part of a group or organization	0	2	5	0	0	0	0	0
Help produce clean movies	0	0	2	3	0	0	0	0
Totals	0	2	12	8	19	15	9	0

TABLE A-34
Clergy and Lay Attitudes on Premarital and Extramarital Sex, By Type and Degree of Religious Commitment

Sample	Index	Ranking	Sexual relations before marriage with intended spouse all right. (Agreeing)	By Percentage Premarital sexual relations lead to serious emotional difficulties in marriage. (Agreeing)	Particular situation could justify extramarital relations. (Agreeing)
Clergy	Beliefs	Low	26	63	58
		Moderate	19	38	22
		High	4	31	5
			$(p = .01)$	$(p = .001)$	$(p = .001)$
Lay	Beliefs	Low	20	47	27
		Moderate	15	38	22
		High	7	30	14
			$(p = .01)$	$(p = .001)$	$(p = .01)$
Lay	Associational Involvement	Low	22	49	26
		Moderate	10	34	18
		High	9	31	18
			$(p = .01)$	$(p = .001)$	$(p = NS)$
Lay	Communal Involvement	Low	17	43	24
		Moderate	14	38	19
		High	6	27	24
			$(p = .05)$	$(p = .001)$	$(p = NS)$

Lay	Practices			
	Low	20	49	24
	Moderate	13	35	22
	High	8	30	15
		(p = .01)	(p = .001)	(p = .05)
Lay	Knowledge			
	Low	17	40	28
	Moderate	14	40	23
	High	11	34	15
		(p = NS)	(p = NS)	(p = .01)

The Lutheran Ethic

TABLE A-35

Clergy and Laymen Who Take Action Against Violence and Sex in Movies and on TV, By Type and Degree of Religious Commitment

Sample	Index	Ranking	Have tried to do something about it. (By Percentage)
Clergy	Beliefs ($p = .001$)	Low	53
		Moderate	53
		High	80
Lay	Beliefs ($p = $ NS)	Low	22
		Moderate	19
		High	24
Lay	Associational Involvement ($p = $ NS)	Low	18
		Moderate	21
		High	24
Lay	Communal Involvement ($p = $ NS)	Low	20
		Moderate	23
		High	18
Lay	Practices ($p = .01$)	Low	15
		Moderate	19
		High	28
Lay	Knowledge ($p = .001$)	Low	12
		Moderate	18
		High	31

TABLE A-36

Validation of the New Morality Index (Lutheran Clergy)

	Ranking By Percentage		
	Low	Moderate	High
In the area of sex relations, traditional religious standards are no longer adequate. (Agreeing) $p = .001$	20	31	74
I look upon the "new morality" as a device of Satan to undermine the consciousness of sin. (Disagreeing) $p = .001$	23	38	84
A woman should have the right to get an abortion if she does not want to bring a child into the world. (Agreeing) p = .001	8	12	40

TABLE A-37

Laymen Ranking Low on the New Morality Index, By Ranking on the Religious Practices Index, Controlled for Social Class

Class	Ranking on Practices Index	*By Percentage* Ranking Low on New Morality Index
Lower	Low	36
	Moderate	45
	High	54
Middle	Low	35
	Moderate	37
	High	53
Upper	Low	18
	Moderate	29
	High	31

TABLE A-38

Clergy and Lay Attitudes on Sex in Marriage, Traditional Religious Sex Standards, and the Teaching of Methods of Birth Control, By Type and Degree of Religious Commitment

By Percentage

Sample	Index	Ranking	Sexual relations between husband and wife should be carried out with restraint. (Agreeing)	In sex relations, traditional religious standards are no longer adequate. (Disagreeing)	Sex education in high school should include methods of birth control. (Disagreeing)
Clergy	Beliefs	Low	9	25	9
		Moderate	26	60	19
		High	23	84	52
			($p = .05$)	($p = .001$)	($p = .001$)
Lay	Beliefs	Low	32	46	23
		Moderate	41	54	31
		High	39	62	46
			($p = .05$)	($p = .001$)	($p = .001$)
Lay	Associational Involvement	Low	35	52	29
		Moderate	40	51	35
		High	40	61	37
			($p = \text{NS}$)	($p = .05$)	($p = .05$)
Lay	Communal Involvement	Low	34	54	28
		Moderate	36	53	34
		High	48	61	43
			($p = .01$)	($p = .05$)	($p = .01$)

Lay				
Practices	Low	40	52	29
	Moderate	35	54	33
	High	39	58	39
		(p = NS)	(p = NS)	(p = .05)

Lay				
Knowledge	Low	46	51	32
	Moderate	41	53	34
	High	31	59	35
		(p = .01)	(p = .05)	(p = NS)

TABLE A-39

Lay and Clergy Suggested Actions to Be Taken By the Church in Lowering the Death Rate from Automobile Accidents

By Percentage

Suggested Action	Lay LCA	ALC	MS	WS	Clergy LCA	ALC	MS	WS
(N)	(67)	(85)	(72)	(62)	(45)	(47)	(108)	(12)
Actions Within Local Congregation or the Institution of Religion								
Talk, discuss with individuals or groups	11	9	10	7	0	4	4	0
Produce written literature	4	2	4	0	0	4	4	0
Sermons (general)	24	30	23	20	0	2	8	0
Sermons against alcoholism	5	6	6	10	2	0	2	0
General education, instruction, teaching	11	8	11	7	4	6	6	0
Educate young people	11	6	6	10	2	0	1	0
Teach responsible Christian behavior, fairness, tolerance, etc.	11	13	12	8	32	30	30	17
Stress Fifth Commandment	2	11	6	13	14	32	22	58
Show movies	0	0	3	3	2	2	0	0
Sponsor programs and speakers	2	3	1	2	13	6	2	0
Get people to attend church	2	0	0	0	0	0	0	0

Stress obedience to traffic laws	7	5	7	15	7	0	8	17
Keep reminding people of accidents	2	2	3	2	4	0	6	0
Pray	0	0	4	0	0	0	1	0
Preach Gospel	0	0	0	0	0	2	0	0
Have a traffic safety Sunday	0	0	1	0	0	0	0	8
Totals	92	95	97	99	80	88	94	100

Actions to be Taken Outside of the Local Congregation and the Institution of Religion

Work for better safety legislation	5	0	0	2	11	9	4	0
Work for safer cars	0	3	0	0	4	0	2	0
Work for better law enforcement	1	0	0	0	0	2	0	0
Work to get unsafe drivers off the road	2	2	3	0	0	0	0	0
Work for better transportation system, planning	0	0	0	0	4	0	0	0
Totals	8	5	3	4	19	11	6	0

TABLE A-40

What Lutheran Laymen and Clergy Feel is "Very Important" for a Lutheran to Believe or Do, By Type and Degree of Religious Commitment

By Percentage

Sample	Index	Ranking	Accept all church creeds and doctrines	Attend church every Sunday	Be active in church activities and organizations	Pray daily	Work for social justice	Read the Bible daily	Tithe (give 10% of income)	Be a member of your particular branch of Lutheranism	Participate regularly in Communion
Clergy	Beliefs	Low	8	53	12	65	79	42	15	5	85
		Moderate	38	48	19	87	58	65	32	13	93
		High	70	90	37	98	51	85	38	37	97
		(p)	(.001)	(.001)	(.001)	(.001)	(.05)	(.001)	(.05)	(.001)	(NS)
Lay	Beliefs	Low	32	35	26	63	53	29	27	27	65
		Moderate	63	68	46	89	53	62	40	45	91
		High	73	82	57	97	48	82	52	62	98
		(p)	(.001)	(.001)	(.001)	(.001)	(NS)	(.001)	(.001)	(.001)	(.001)

Lay	Associational Involvement	Low	53	51	27	77	46	42	31	38	76
		Moderate	61	59	42	85	55	63	45	47	87
		High	62	80	63	93	54	74	45	52	95
		(p)	(.05)	(.001)	(.001)	(.001)	(NS)	(.001)	(.01)	(.01)	(.001)
Lay	Communal Involvement	Low	53	56	38	78	58	52	38	43	81
		Moderate	56	62	43	87	47	58	37	42	87
		High	74	82	64	93	54	79	53	62	95
		(p)	(.01)	(.001)	(.001)	(.001)	(NS)	(.001)	(.01)	(.001)	(.01)
Lay	Practices	Low	49	50	33	71	45	43	33	31	76
		Moderate	59	62	40	86	50	59	38	46	87
		High	67	79	60	97	59	77	50	59	96
		(p)	(.001)	(.001)	(.001)	(.001)	(.01)	(.001)	(.01)	(.001)	(.001)
Lay	Knowledge	Low	68	65	43	78	51	52	41	47	83
		Moderate	53	57	42	82	52	56	40	44	84
		High	58	70	48	93	52	69	40	46	91
		(p)	(NS)	(.05)	(NS)	(.01)	(NS)	(.001)	(NS)	(NS)	(.05)

TABLE A-41

Clergy and Lay Attitudes on the Role of Clergymen, By Type and Degree of Religious Commitment

Sample	Index	Ranking	Should participate in protest demonstrations. (Disagreeing)	By Percentage Should stick to religion, not concern themselves with social, economic, political problems. (Agreeing)	If clergymen picket or demonstrate members can withhold or limit contributions. (Agreeing)
Clergy	Beliefs	Low	8	2	12
		Moderate	32	13	16
		High	68	32	25
			($p = .001$)	($p = .001$)	($p = .05$)
Lay	Beliefs	Low	69	48	39
		Moderate	72	52	35
		High	80	61	32
			($p = .05$)	($p = .01$)	($p = $ NS)
Lay	Associational Involvement	Low	74	56	54
		Moderate	72	53	52
		High	74	52	50
			($p = $ NS)	($p = $ NS)	($p = $ NS)
Lay	Communal Involvement	Low	68	50	29
		Moderate	74	53	36
		High	83	53	36
			($p = .01$)	($p = .01$)	($p = .01$)

Lay	Practices			
	Low	72	53	38
	Moderate	74	55	32
	High	74	53	36
		(p = NS)	(p = NS)	(p = NS)

Lay	Knowledge			
	Low	77	61	41
	Moderate	74	47	37
	High	70	56	30
		(p = NS)	(p = .05)	(p = .05)

TABLE A-42

Clergy and Lay Attitudes on Role of the Congregation,
By Type and Degree of Religious Commitment

| | | | By Percentage | |
Sample	Index	Ranking	All congregations should support special ministry. (Disagreeing)	Primary responsibility is needs of own membership. (Agreeing)	Local church should make decisions without interference from synod or district. (Agreeing)
Clergy	Beliefs	Low	8	17	21
		Moderate	9	46	48
		High	17	54	50
			(p = .05)	(p = .001)	(p = .001)
Lay	Beliefs	Low	9	70	75
		Moderate	10	69	50
		High	22	77	42
			(p = .01)	(p = .05)	(p = .001)
Lay	Associational Involvement	Low	12	72	58
		Moderate	13	75	49
		High	15	70	47
			(p = NS)	(p = NS)	(p = .05)
Lay	Communal Involvement	Low	10	67	53
		Moderate	13	72	51
		High	20	82	51
			(p = .05)	(p = .01)	(p = NS)

Lay	Practices			
	Low	13	71	60
	Moderate	12	72	48
	High	15	74	46
		(p = NS)	(p = NS)	(p = .01)

Lay	Knowledge			
	Low	12	73	60
	Moderate	14	73	52
	High	13	71	45
		(p = NS)	(p = NS)	(p = .01)

TABLE A-43

*Clergy and Lay Attitudes on the Church's Playing a Role in Reducing
Automobile Deaths, By Type and Degree of Religious Commitment*

Sample	Index	Ranking	By Percentage Church as role in lowering accident rate. (Agreeing)
Clergy	Beliefs ($p = $ NS)	Low Moderate High	92 94 88
Lay	Beliefs ($p = .05$)	Low Moderate High	33 36 41
Lay	Associational Involvement ($p = .001$)	Low Moderate High	26 35 47
Lay	Communal Involvement ($p = $ NS)	Low Moderate High	33 38 36
Lay	Practices ($p = .001$)	Low Moderate High	29 36 44
Lay	Knowledge ($p = .001$)	Low Moderate High	27 33 46

TABLE A-44

Validation of the Social Action Index (Lay Data)

	Ranking, By Percentage		
	Low	Moderate	High
Do you think the church should do anything about the sale of guns in our society? (Yes) $p = .001$	16	30	42
Rather than just preaching about sin, the church ought to seek, through organized social action, to change the specific social conditions which produce sin. (Agreeing) $p = .001$	48	70	82
It is all right for ministers and other religious leaders to march and participate in protest demonstration. (Agreeing) $p = .001$	15	30	60
It is not as important to worry about life after death as about what one can do in this life. (Agreeing) $p = .001$	41	57	67
The Christian faith should be less concerned with sacraments and more concerned with expressions of love and concern for social justice. (Agreeing) $p = .001$	25	38	70

289

The Lutheran Ethic

TABLE A-45

Clergy and Lay Attitudes on Civil Disobedience,
By Type and Degree of Religious Commitment

Sample	Index	Ranking	By Percentage Lutherans should obey secular authorities or state and not break laws. (Agreeing)
Clergy	Beliefs ($p = .001$)	Low	20
		Moderate	39
		High	68
Lay	Beliefs ($p = .01$)	Low	68
		Moderate	83
		High	81
Lay	Associational Involvement ($p = .05$)	Low	74
		Moderate	80
		High	81
Lay	Communal Involvement ($p = .05$)	Low	76
		Moderate	78
		High	85
Lay	Practices ($p = $ NS)	Low	74
		Moderate	80
		High	81
Lay	Knowledge ($p = $ NS)	Low	77
		Moderate	76
		High	82

TABLE A-46

Lay and Clergy Reactions to the Present State of Race Relations, By Type and Degree of Religious Commitment

Sample	Index	Ranking	Treat only in sermons and/or study groups.	By Percentage Individuals active, but church not involved.	Both individuals and churches active.
Clergy	Beliefs ($p = .001$)	Low	3	9	85
		Moderate	7	36	57
		High	11	60	23
Lay	Beliefs ($p = NS$)	Low	18	53	27
		Moderate	22	43	33
		High	25	49	24
Lay	Associational Involvement ($p = NS$)	Low	23	49	27
		Moderate	23	46	30
		High	21	47	31
Lay	Communal Involvement ($p = NS$)	Low	25	42	32
		Moderate	21	49	29
		High	20	54	23
Lay	Practices ($p = NS$)	Low	21	51	28
		Moderate	24	47	27
		High	23	44	32
Lay	Knowledge ($p = .05$)	Low	28	46	24
		Moderate	24	47	28
		High	16	50	33

TABLE A-47

Clergy and Lay Attitudes Toward Worship Services, By Type and Degree of Religious Commitment

By Percentage

Sample	Index	Ranking	Liturgy, services, and hymns should be changed to attract new members from different social classes. (Disagreeing)	Like service with extensive liturgy and formality. (Disagreeing)	Like hymns as they are now.	Church is organized and services conducted in way commanded by God. (Agreeing)
Clergy	Beliefs	Low	26	*	14	*
		Moderate	25	*	19	*
		High	34	*	29	*
			(p = .05)		(p = .05)	
Lay	Beliefs	Low	74	59	65	41
		Moderate	80	48	73	68
		High	90	48	82	71
			(p = .001)	(p = .05)	(p = .001)	(p = .001)
Lay	Associational Involvement	Low	79	55	71	60
		Moderate	79	53	73	62
		High	86	46	78	65
			(p = NS)	(p = .05)	(p = .05)	(p = NS)
Lay	Communal Involvement	Low	78	52	73	57
		Moderate	83	54	73	59
		High	85	42	80	80
			(p = NS)	(p = .05)	(p = NS)	(p = .01)

Lay	Practices	Low	81	55	69	54
		Moderate	80	52	78	64
		High	83	47	75	69
			(p = NS)	(p = .05)	(p = .05)	(p = .01)
Lay	Knowledge	Low	77	44	73	77
		Moderate	82	54	77	57
		High	85	53	71	57
			(p = NS)	(p = .05)	(p = NS)	(p = .001)

*Not asked of clergy

TABLE A-48

*Lay and Clergy Attitudes on Change in the Institution of Religion,
By Type and Degree of Religious Commitment*

Sample	Index	Ranking	By Percentage Important to carry out Lutheran traditions. (Agreeing)
Clergy	Beliefs ($p = .05$)	Low	2
		Moderate	8
		High	14
Lay	Beliefs ($p = .001$)	Low	27
		Moderate	43
		High	65
Lay	Associational Involvement ($p = .01$)	Low	39
		Moderate	47
		High	51
Lay	Communal Involvement ($p = .001$)	Low	42
		Moderate	43
		High	61
Lay	Practices ($p = .001$)	Low	38
		Moderate	45
		High	54
Lay	Knowledge ($p = $ NS)	Low	49
		Moderate	41
		High	48

TABLE A-49

Clergy and Lay Attitudes on Church Doctrines and Creeds,
By Type and Degree of Religious Commitment

Sample	Index	Ranking	Creeds can be expected to change over time. (Disagreeing)	Many doctrines have little relevance to modern world. (Disagreeing)
Clergy	Beliefs	Low	14	38
		Moderate	49	78
		High	72	94
		$(p = .001)$		
			$(p = .001)$	$(p = .001)$
Lay	Beliefs	Low	25	61
		Moderate	29	71
		High	58	76
			$(p = .001)$	$(p = .01)$
Lay	Associational Involvement	Low	32	66
		Moderate	40	70
		High	52	73
			$(p = .001)$	$(p = NS)$
Lay	Communal Involvement	Low	33	70
		Moderate	43	71
		High	53	68
			$(p = .001)$	$(p = NS)$
Lay	Practices	Low	36	65
		Moderate	37	72
		High	52	73
			$(p = .001)$	$(p = .05)$
Lay	Knowledge	Low	30	57
		Moderate	38	73
		High	53	76
			$(p = .001)$	$(p = .001)$

By Percentage

TABLE A-50

Validation of the Images of Man Index (Clergy Data)

	By Percentage		
	Low	Moderate	High
Man by himself is incapable of anything but sin. (Agree or Probably Agree) $p = .001$	13	29	68
I see unconverted man as created by God but controlled by sin; his behavior is neither directed by God nor is he in complete control of his own life. (Agree or Probably Agree) $p = .001$	27	58	77

TABLE A-51

Lay and Clergy Optimistic or Pessimistic Orientations Toward Life,
By Type and Degree of Religious Commitment

Sample	Index	Ranking	*By Percentage* Man may solve his problems on earth and live in a peaceful world. (Disagreeing)
Clergy	Beliefs ($p = .001$)	Low	76
		Moderate	93
		High	98
Lay	Beliefs ($p = .001$)	Low	52
		Moderate	59
		High	71
Lay	Associational Involvement ($p = .05$)	Low	58
		Moderate	61
		High	66
Lay	Communal Involvement ($p = NS$)	Low	57
		Moderate	64
		High	64
Lay	Practices ($p = .05$)	Low	58
		Moderate	60
		High	67
Lay	Knowledge ($p = .001$)	Low	47
		Moderate	61
		High	72

TABLE A-52

Validation of the God's Will Versus Man's Will Index (Lay Data)

| | Ranking By Percentage | | |
	Low	Moderate	High
The separation of men into classes and groups is the direct result of God's will and should not be tampered with. (Agreeing) $p = .001$)	10	23	40
Since there is always going to be poverty, it's foolish for the government to spend so much money to try and rid the world of it. (Agreeing) $p = .001$)	18	26	30
Today God is using individuals and nations to carry out His continuing punishment against the Jews. (Agreeing) $p = .001$	6	11	20
Because of the religious nature of marriage, sexual relations between husband and wife should be carried out with restraint. (Agreeing) $p = .001$	28	42	50
It is right that convicted murderers should be given the death penalty. (Agreeing) $p = .001$	29	43	56

TABLE A-53

*Clergy and Lay Attitudes Toward Childrearing,
By Type and Degree of Religious Commitment*

Sample	Index	Ranking	To obey	Most Important, By Percentage To think for himself	To work hard	To help others
Clergy	Beliefs ($p = .001$)	Low	6	56	2	36
		Moderate	17	50	5	28
		High	52	32	5	11
Lay	Beliefs ($p = .001$)	Low	13	73	8	6
		Moderate	23	59	6	12
		High	33	51	6	10
Lay	Associational Involvement ($p = $ NS)	Low	20	64	7	9
		Moderate	25	60	5	10
		High	27	57	6	10
Lay	Communal Involvement ($p = $ NS)	Low	24	61	5	10
		Moderate	22	63	6	9
		High	30	51	8	11
Lay	Practices ($p = .01$)	Low	18	67	6	9
		Moderate	23	58	9	10
		High	30	56	4	10
Lay	Knowledge ($p = .01$)	Low	32	51	7	10
		Moderate	21	63	6	10
		High	21	64	6	9

The Lutheran Ethic

TABLE A-54

Lay and Clergy Attitudes Regarding Conflicts Between Science and Religion, By Type and Degree of Religious Commitment

Sample	Index	Ranking	By Percentage Conflicts are "very serious" or "somewhat serious." (Agreeing)	Can accept the evolution of man from lower animals. (Disagreeing)
Clergy	Beliefs	Low	15	6
		Moderate	36	52
		High	61	95
			($p = .001$)	($p = .001$)
Lay	Beliefs	Low	39	41
		Moderate	56	64
		High	59	84
			($p = .001$)	($p = .001$)
Lay	Associational Involvement	Low	52	57
		Moderate	53	61
		High	52	75
			($p = $ NS)	($p = .001$)
Lay	Communal Involvement	Low	47	58
		Moderate	51	65
		High	68	75
			($p = .001$)	($p = .001$)
Lay	Practices	Low	48	60
		Moderate	55	61
		High	55	73
			($p = $ NS)	($p = .01$)
Lay	Knowledge	Low	53	48
		Moderate	56	62
		High	49	77
			($p = $ NS)	($p = .001$)

TABLE A-55

Clergy and Lay Rankings on the Salvation Index,
By Type and Degree of Religious Commitment

Sample	Index	Ranking	*By Percentage*		
			Low	Moderate	High
Clergy	Beliefs ($p = .001$)	Low	88	6	6
		Moderate	46	32	22
		High	6	29	65
Lay	Beliefs ($p = .001$)	Low	43	40	17
		Moderate	20	45	35
		High	9	41	50
Lay	Associational Involvement ($p = .01$)	Low	29	41	30
		Moderate	23	41	36
		High	15	45	40
Lay	Communal Involvement ($p = .001$)	Low	29	44	27
		Moderate	22	43	35
		High	13	37	50
Lay	Practices ($p = .001$)	Low	34	40	26
		Moderate	21	41	38
		High	14	46	40
Lay	Knowledge ($p = .01$)	Low	33	46	21
		Moderate	25	41	34
		High	13	41	46

TABLE A-56

What Lutheran Laymen Are Seeking From Their Religion,
By Type and Degree of Religious Commitment

Index of Commitment	Ranking	By Percentage		
		Comfort and security in handling problems	Motivation to reform society	Teachings on how to behave
Beliefs (p = .01)	Low	61	14	25
	Moderate	69	10	21
	High	77	6	17
Associational Involvement (p = .05)	Low	65	9	26
	Moderate	70	9	21
	High	73	12	15
Communal Involvement (p = .01)	Low	65	9	26
	Moderate	69	12	19
	High	81	4	15
Practices (p = NS)	Low	67	9	24
	Moderate	67	12	21
	High	75	8	17
Knowledge (p = NS)	Low	72	7	21
	Moderate	69	11	20
	High	69	10	21

TABLE A-57

*Student Rankings on the Religious Knowledge Index,
By Religious Body*

| | Rankings, By Percentage | | |
	Low	Moderate	High
Jewish	15	36	49
United Church of Christ	15	35	50
United Methodist	9	42	49
Episcopalian	5	47	48
Presbyterian	8	51	41
Roman Catholic	7	37	56
Baptist	4	21	75
LCA	0	33	67
ALC	12	34	54
MS	3	27	70
WS	5	27	68

TABLE A-58
Student Answers to Anti-Semitism Questions

By Percentage

	United Church of Christ	United Methodist	Episcopal	Presbyterian	Roman Catholic	Baptist	LCA	ALC	MS	WS
The Jews can never be forgiven for what they did to Jesus until they accept Him as the true Savior. (Agreeing)	13	14	6	9	10	39	35	19	25	46
The curse which the Jews called down upon themselves after crucifying Jesus still rests on them and their children to this very day. (Agreeing)	9	10	14	13	16	30	27	17	29	44
The reason the Jews have so much trouble is because God is punishing them for rejecting Jesus. (Agreeing)	0	5	3	5	6	22	8	2	10	26
Today God is using individuals and nations to carry out His continuing punishment against the Jews. (Agreeing)	4	3	0	5	4	15	4	6	10	18

*Questions not asked of Jews.

TABLE A-59

Student Rankings on New Morality Index

| | By Percentage | | |
	Low	Moderate	High
Jewish	7	22	71
United Church of Christ	15	29	56
United Methodist	13	30	57
Episcopal	7	27	66
Presbyterian	17	23	60
Roman Catholic	20	33	47
Baptist	31	29	40
LCA	15	33	52
ALC	21	26	53
MS	23	30	47
WS	28	28	44

TABLE A-60

Student Rankings on God's Will Versus Man's Will Index

| | By Percentage | | |
	Low	Moderate	High
Jewish	88	4	8
United Church of Christ	88	6	6
United Methodist	88	8	4
Episcopal	94	3	3
Presbyterian	82	15	3
Roman Catholic	82	13	5
Baptist	72	17	11
LCA	92	4	4
ALC	76	13	11
MS	67	18	15
WS	26	55	19

Index

Lawrence K. Kersten is assistant professor of sociology at Eastern Michigan University and adjunct assistant professor of Urban Planning at the University of Michigan. He was formerly Research Analyst with the Metropolitan Detroit Council of Churches.

The manuscript was edited by Linda Grant. This book and jacket were designed by Joanne Colman. The type face for the text is Baskerville, cut for Mergenthaler linotype in 1931 and based on the designs of John Baskerville in 1757. The display face is Garamond, designed by Claude Garamond, first used in 1620.

Manufactured in the United States of America.